Paraprofessionals and Their Performance

Alan Gartner
foreword by
Frank Riessman

The Praeger Special Studies program—
utilizing the most modern and efficient book
production techniques and a selective
worldwide distribution network—makes
available to the academic, government, and
business communities significant, timely
research in U.S. and international economic, social, and political development.

Paraprofessionals and Their Performance

A Survey of
Education, Health,
and Social Service Programs

PRAEGER SPECIAL STUDIES IN U.S. ECONOMIC AND SOCIAL DEVELOPMENT

Praeger Publishers　　New York　Washington　London

PRAEGER PUBLISHERS
111 Fourth Avenue, New York, N.Y. 10003, U.S.A.
5, Cromwell Place, London S.W.7, England

Published in the United States of America in 1971
by Praeger Publishers, Inc.

Third printing, 1972

Library of Congress Catalog Card Number: 75-150707

Printed in the United States of America

To Audrey

FOREWORD:
THE
PARAPROFESSIONAL
AND
INSTITUTIONAL
CHANGE
by Frank Riessman

This book provides a remarkable integration of a vast array of data on the way in which paraprofessionals contribute to the improvement of human service practice—by reaching hitherto unreached people, by providing new kinds of services, by improving the professional's performance and sometimes his attitudes, and by introducing a new community ethos into agencies that have limited ties to the community.

This study analyzes the research on the paraprofessional in a variety of fields: health, education, social service, corrections, and mental health. It presents a highly balanced picture of the accomplishments of paraprofessional workers and anyone interested in the role of the paraprofessional in current U.S. society should consider it carefully. The author not only covers all the existing literature (which is remarkably extensive), but he also develops important insights regarding a variety of issues, including the relationship of indigeneity and training, the relationship of the paraprofessional and the professional, and the relationship of the paraprofessional and the community.

While no one source reported in this study yields conclusive evidence regarding the effect of paraprofessionals on increased service efficiency, the multiplicity of data garnered by different investigators, with different biases and employing different research tools, add up to quite a convincing picture. This is not to say that paraprofessionals always or necessarily better the performance of the agency, but frequently they do, and with appropriate training they can improve the service considerably.

However, this is only one dimension of the responsibility the paraprofessional has been asked to assume. The book deals penetratingly with some of the other dimensions, including the role of the paraprofessional in introducing social and institutional change, in reducing poverty, in affecting colleges and credential practices, in reducing manpower shortages, and in stimulating significant upgrading and new careers.

We believe that the rapid acceptance of the paraprofessional by the professionals and the agencies is related to the crisis in professional practice produced by the highly vocal demands of the poor and the minorities. These demands, arising initially from the Black movement, are expressed specifically in the community-control movement which calls for accountability, relevance, and revitalization of the services. Starting in the schools and spreading to the health agencies and other human service sectors, the poor are refusing to accept the professional's explanation for failure to deliver adequate service.

In this context, for example, it is easy to understand why teachers who might have been resistant to the idea of accepting aides in large numbers quickly responded to the idea of paraprofessionals assisting them in relating to the community, understanding the community, and in some cases, warding off the community, to say nothing of dealing with youngsters who were giving them lots of trouble in the classroom. While there is a great deal of talk about the value of paraprofessionals in reducing manpower shortages, it is unlikely that this was a crucial element in curtailing professional resistance; it is only in the health field, with the acceptance of paramedics, that the manpower issue may be decisive.

It might have been easy to predict that paraprofessionals would be coopted by the agencies to become miniature professionals and play the role of buffer with the community, but there is considerable evidence that nothing so simple occurred. In fact, in some cases, the paraprofessionals seem to have played a role in radicalizing the professionals—sometimes uniting with the student and professional forces and sometimes leading them. Thus, the role of paraprofessionals at Lincoln Hospital Mental Health Services in the Bronx and at Topeka, Kansas, has had a national impact in relation to radical demands for institutional change, particularly for worker participation in agency decisions, sometimes called worker control. In Topeka, the paraprofessionals led the demand for change in mental-health hospitals with their slogan "We Care" and with the tactic of a "work-in" rather than a strike, because they were concerned with the continuance of service ("we serve") to the community.[1]

A most striking statement of the paraprofessionals' concern for their community and for social change is evidenced in the words of the workers themselves:

> We entered the New Careers program enthusiastic about the prospect of achieving the bright goals on our agenda. But when the newness of the job placement and the educational aspect of the program wore off, we were able to see the fallacies and contradictions with which we had to deal. First of all, we had to decide whether we were going to accept things as they were or try to effect a change. Some of the things that caused us stress were lack of a career ladder, no salary range, and lack of understanding of what was expected of us on the job. It became apparent we had a fight on our hands if we wanted our program to succeed. We enlisted the guidance and advice of our instructors in Human Relationships, Clinical Conference, and, most importantly, Social Systems. It was there we learned how to intervene successfully in a system.
>
> To avoid falling into the same bag that other community professionals have, we must be constantly aware of our ultimate goal: to get the Black community on its feet economically and medically. The only way that we can do this is not to allow ourselves to be sucked into the Establishment. We must not allow the Establishment to use us to pacify the community. We must always

work for the common good of our people, not becoming flunkies doing the dirty work of our agency to "cool out" the poor, especially Blacks. We must continually intervene in systems that are not truly concerned about the welfare of our people.

We are aware that the war isn't over just because we have won a battle. We must continue to fight each new encounter as if it was the first. However, we must not become paranoid in thinking that every confrontation is a fighting situation.[2]

And the psychiatrist, Salvador Minuchin, states the role of the paraprofessional in the mental health field as a social change agent in another way:

the inclusion of paraprofessionals in the existing structures of delivery of service brought to a head a bipolarity of approaches to mental illness which was already incipient in the field.[3]

The bipolarity refers to the activist, sociological emphasis on the one hand and the more traditional, internally oriented approach on the other. But the significant point is the role ascribed to the paraprofessional as a strategic catalyst in the field of mental health.

Minuchin's observations, Charles G. Grosser's study, as well as a number of others indicate that paraprofessionals can have a significant impact on professionals, professional practice, and professional-service delivery.[4]

There is evidence from the Minneapolis study cited in this volume that the longer the paraprofessional works in the agency, the more he becomes committed to the community, and, in a study by Frederick L. Ahearn, Jr., the more militant he becomes.[5]

Paraprofessionals do not appear to become less active in their community organizations as was presumed by some critics. The study by Marilyn Gittell shows there were more of them involved on antipoverty boards and on community boards in the Demonstration Districts in New York City.[6]

It should be noted, however, that the influence of paraprofessionals on work systems frequently occurs in a different manner than through community boards that function outside the work place. Paraprofessionals work inside the system, and as one Black leader put it, "I would rather have them working on the inside than cheering on the outside." They learn the technology and norms of the system and how the system needs to be changed. Moreover, they have the potential of using very different although complementary (to the community) ways of changing it.[7]

Perhaps most significant, paraprofessionals have recognized that it is impossible to win their demands for new careers, upgrading, and institutional change in the agencies and training institutions without becoming organized. This study indicates that they are joining unions in large numbers, such as the American Federation of Teachers, the American Federation of State, County, and Municipal Employees, the Drug and Hospital Workers Union (1199) and the Social Service Employees Union. They have won many demands for career ladders, upgrading, release time for education, and perhaps are beginning to change the character and ethos of some unions and affect such so-called old nonprofessionals as nurses aides who are now also demanding upgrading and so forth.

Paraprofessionals have also won considerable attention (and membership) in such professional organizations as the American Public Health Association, the American Public Welfare Association, the American Orthopsychiatric Association, the Vocational Rehabilitation Association, the National Education Association, and the National Association of Social Workers. They are providing a new voice in these organizations and are raising questions about traditional licensing, training practice, and service delivery.

In another and much more indirect way, paraprofessionals may be playing an important role in beginning to increase general understanding that poor people, who were previously thought of as unemployable, can very quickly perform highly useful public service. To some extent this may have an impact on the acceptance of large public-service programs such as those being considered in Congress where government employment is being seen as *employment of first resort* rather than last resort.

It is impossible to understand the paraprofessional movement unless it is seen in relation to a whole series of new trends relating to credentialism and professionalism, including the new external degree, the concern for recurrent education, the expanded work-study programs in colleges, and the demand for more relevance in college courses. Thus, paraprofessionals working in a variety of ways and in concert with other forces (open enrollment, community control, and so forth) seem to be having an impact on institutional change in colleges, in credentialing and training systems, in agencies and schools, and perhaps finally on governmental policy and legislation.

While this book focuses on the paraprofessionals' effects on human-service practice and productivity, it also furnishes ample evidence regarding their role in social change.

NOTES

1. Alex Efthim, " 'We Care' in Kansas: The Nonprofessionals Revolt," *Nation* (August 5, 1968), 18-21.

2. Roberta Boyette *et al.*, "The Plight of the New Careerist," *American Journal of Orthopsychiatry*, XLI, 2 (March, 1971), 237-38.

3. Salvador Minuchin, "The Paraprofessional and the Use of Confrontation in the Mental Health Field," *American Journal of Orthopsychiatry*, XXXIX, 5 (October, 1969), 726.

4. Charles G. Grosser, *The Role of the Nonprofessional in the Manpower Development Program*. Washington, D.C.: U.S. Department of Labor, 1966.

5. Margaret A. Thompson, "Contamination of New Careerists by Professionalization: Fact or Fancy?" Minneapolis: New Careers Research,

University of Minnesota, 1969; Frederick L. Ahearn, Jr., "Paraprofessionals: Anomie and Activism," paper presented at the National Conference of Social Welfare, Chicago, June 1, 1970.

6. "Report of the Institute for Community Studies," Queens College, N.Y., November, 1970.

7. Alan Gartner and Frank Riessman, "The New Careers Strategy for Changing the Professions," a chapter to appear in *The New Professionals*, edited by Ronald Gross and Paul Osterman, to be published by Simon and Schuster, 1971.

ACKNOWLEDGMENTS

Anyone who works in this field cannot be without debt to Frank Riessman both for his initial formulations (along with Arthur Pearl) and his ongoing contributions. Also, we are indebted to Vivian Carter Jackson and Ralph Acosta along with our other colleagues at the New Careers Training Laboratory and the New Careers Development Center.

A book of this sort relies basically on the work of many people throughout the country. Many persons who already carry the heavy load of launching and operating a complex and often innovative program have taken the time to keep records and report on both successes and failures. Without them, this book would not have been possible and, to them, we are deeply grateful. Harriet Johnson has diligently sought out many of these studies and has gone back to the journals again and again to find the "one last reference."

Our Center has been the recipient since 1967 of a number of grants which have enabled us to collect much of the data used in this book. Among the grant sources, we are particularly grateful to the Ford Foundation and Basil Whiting; the U.S. Office of Education and Don Davies, William Smith, Wilton Anderson, and Bill Berndt; and the National Center for Health Services, Research, and Development and Benjamin Alexander; as well as New York University and Sidney Roth.

Both Harold J. Gartner and Jack and Aranka Joseph kindly provided an opportunity for the writing of the book. Marilyn Boyce bore with a handwriting that sometimes compared unfavorably with hieroglyphics and insertions and amendations that often exceeded the text.

The dedication of this book to Audrey Gartner is but a minimal expression of her contribution to this book and all else. Of course, neither she nor anyone other than the author bears responsibility for what is presented here.

CONTENTS

LIST OF TABLES

LIST OF ABBREVIATIONS

ABE	Adult Basic Education
AFSCME	American Federation of State, County, and Municipal Employees
AFT	American Federation of Teachers
APHA	American Public Health Association
APWA	American Public Welfare Association
CAP	Community Action Program
CSO	Community service officer
CWSE	Council of Social Work Education
ESEA	Elementary and Secondary Education Act
ETS	Education Testing Service
GED	General Education Diploma
HARYOU	Harlem Youth Opportunities Program
HEP	High School Equivalency Program
HEW	U.S. Department of Health, Education, and Welfare
HUD	U.S. Department of Housing and Urban Development
LANCO	Los Angeles New Careers Organization
LHMHS	Lincoln Hospital Mental Health Services
LPN	Licensed Practical Nurse
MCEP	Manhattan Court Employment Project
MDTA	Manpower Development and Training Act
MFY	Mobilization for Youth
NASW	National Association of Social Workers
NEA	National Education Association
NIMH	National Institute of Mental Health
OEO	Office of Economic Opportunity
ojt	On-the-job training
PA	Physician's assistant
PSCP	Public Service Careers Program
RN	Registered nurse
RODEO	Reeducation of Delinquency Through Expansion of Opportunity
STAR	Supplementary Teaching in Advanced Reading
TAP	Teacher Aide Program
UFT	United Federation of Teachers
VA	Veterans' Administration

Paraprofessionals and
Their Performance

1

INTRODUCTION

The decade of the 1960's was many things and included the hope of John F. Kennedy, bright and then dashed; the civil-rights movement moving North, flourishing and then splintering; the discovery of poverty, the announcement of a war, and the mounting of a skirmish. Connected to each of these was a new concern for the quality of life, particularly as it was affected by the schools and health and welfare institutions. As the concern for increased and new services grew, so too grew a realization that existing manpower resources were inadequate both in numbers and ability to serve the poor. Thus, along with the concern for new services came an interest in new manpower, particularly from among those with less formal training.

The very titling of these new workers gives some hint of the progressive development since the post-World War II years. Aides, nonprofessionals, auxiliaries, and even subprofessionals were common usage in the few programs prior to 1960 and continued to be common usage into the mid-1960's. By that time, although the earlier titles persisted, new forms came to the fore and included paraprofessional, community worker, new careerist, new professional, and community teacher. In part, these new titles reflected little more than their coiners' desire to ascribe status to the new workers. But they also signified two key changes of the middle and late 1960's, the connection of these workers to the local community in which they worked and the incorporation of a career component. We will use the term paraprofessional as, in a sense, the least bad of several poor alternatives. It is perhaps the most commonly used title at present and has, for us, the advantage of neither signifying any one sector of the human services nor any one funding source or program design.

EARLY PARAPROFESSIONAL PROGRAMS

The use of paraprofessionals existed in the settlement-house developments at Henry Street and Hull House and the YMCA's Chicago Area Project.[1]

Several of the New Deal programs, notably the Social Security Act of 1935, the Works Progress Administration, and the National Youth Administration used paraprofessionals, although only the Social Security program survived World War II.[2] There is little discussion of such programs in the professional literature of the 1940's; illustrative of that which occurs is the description of a teacher-aide program in Montana designed to offset wartime shortages.[3]

A continuing concern for meeting manpower shortages characterized the programs of the 1950's. The most prominent, perhaps, was the Ford Foundation supported effort in the public schools of Bay City, Michigan, which later spread to Fairfield, Connecticut, Rutgers, New Jersey, and Newton, Massachusetts.[4] So too, in health and social work, efforts were made to meet professional shortages by recruiting women with college degrees (or at least those who had attended college) but who lacked formal professional training.[5] Another source for new manpower was sought through the upgrading of workers already present, as was done in the California and Maryland state mental-health programs where advanced psychiatric aides were given special training.[6]

Persons from among the population to be served (as had been the case with the Chicago Area Project), were employed in the New York State Youth Board's "Club Project" and several health-education programs to serve Indians, Canadian Eskimos, and migrant workers in Florida.[7] This trend of using workers from among the group to be served continued with such programs as Philadelphia's Great Cities School Improvement Project and Pittsburgh's Team Teaching Project, both begun in 1960; the programs established under the Juvenile and Youth Offenders Control Act of 1961, and the Federal Migrant Health Act of 1962.[8] However, for the first two or three years of the 1960's, the main thrust continued to be in the recruitment of largely middle-class persons to supplement the work of trained professionals. This practice is seen in the recommendations of the Arden House Conference on Casework with the Aging (1960), the National Institute of Mental Health's (NIMH) funded Mental Health Counselors Program (1960), the use of college graduates as social-work assistants in a Cleveland private agency serving the aged (1961), the Chicago Travelers Aid Project (1962), the recommendations of the National Association of Social Workers (NASW) Subcommittee on the Utilization of Personnel (1962), the Veteran's Administration Pilot Study on the Use of Social Work Assistants (1962), and the use of volunteer college students as companions to hospitalized schizophrenics and as volunteer teachers for emotionally disturbed children.[9]

THE INDIGENOUS PARAPROFESSIONAL

In 1963, the first major programs were funded under the President's Committee on Juvenile Delinquency and Youth Crime. Most important of these in terms of our concerns was Mobilization for Youth (MFY), located in New York City's Lower East Side.[10] Delinquents had been used in earlier programs to work with older delinquents.[11] However, MFY added the use of indigenous persons in school and community work, all in a context set by Richard A. Cloward and Lloyd E. Ohlin's "opportunity theory."[12] Some months after MFY began, Frank Riessman viewed the program and found the indigenous workers one of the two most successful aspects of the project (the other being the "helper-therapy" principle); it led him to make the first published call for what he termed "the new nonprofessional."[13]

At about the same time, the staff of the Center for Youth and Community Studies at Howard University began to train young people from impoverished backgrounds for paraprofessional jobs in such human-service fields as child and health care, community organization, recreation, and research.[14]

By 1964, a rash of projects were underway using what Robert Reiff was then calling the "indigenous nonprofessional.[15] These included the New York State Division of Youth's Youth Worker Training Project which used school dropouts and rehabilitated offenders; the New Careers Development Project, funded by NIMH, which trained eighteen inmates in a California prison as program developers; and Project CAUSE, a summer program of the U.S. Department of Labor which trained 1,750 nonprofessionals to staff Youth Opportunity Centers as counselor aides and youth advisers.[16] Of course, 1964 saw the launching of the Office of Economic Opportunity (OEO), which was soon to become the largest employer of paraprofessionals. By June 30, 1965, the end of OEO's first fiscal year, over 25,000 paraprofessionals were employed in community action programs, and over 46,000 in Head Start.[17]

The emphasis on using paraprofessionals recruited from the population to be served reached a new level in 1965 with the publication of *New Careers for the Poor,* which gave the effort a brand name, a guidebook, and in its authors, Arthur Pearl and Frank Riessman, its outspoken advocates. Both had been involved in several of the earlier program efforts described above. Pearl had worked for the New York State Youth Board and was a founder of the Howard University program, while Riessman had worked at Mobilization for Youth and became codirector of the Neighborhood Service Center Program, Lincoln Hospital Mental Health Services (LHMHS).

NEW CAREERS

The Economic Opportunity Act of 1964 provided a dual basis for the expansion of paraprofessional programs. Its charge to provide services to the poor also offered an arena in which they could be employed, especially as the key title (II A) of the act was to be implemented with "maximum feasible participation" of those to be served. And a third basis grew out of the funding in January, 1965, of LHMHS, which coincided with the arrival in Congress of Representative James Scheuer, who served the South Bronx district which encompassed the catchment area of LHMHS. His exposure to the program prompted Congressman Scheuer to propose (on March 1, 1966) the Career Opportunity Act. A week after Scheuer introduced the bill, Riessman, then codirector of LHMHS's Neighborhood Service Center Program, in outlining the features such a bill should include, illustrated how far the conception had gone from the programs of the early 1960's. In responding to the Congressman's request for comments, Riessman urged inclusion in the bill of provision for the following:

1. Entry to college programs in order to "provide credentials for the aides"
2. Employment of nonprofessionals as trainers
3. Inclusion of aides in police, corrections, and research work, in addition to health, education, and welfare programs
4. Development of training curricula
5. Assistance to agencies employing nonprofessionals
6. Changes in civil service regulations
7. A different kind of on-the-job training (ojt) than the usual ojt design
8. Consideration of a nonprofessional college
9. Including nonprofessionals in other programs such as Model Cities and New Towns.[18]

Scheuer's bill was referred to the House Antipoverty Subcommittee where it was combined with a proposal made the previous year by Senator Gaylord Nelson for a rural training and employment program.[19] The new, combined Nelson-Scheuer Amendment to the Economic Opportunity Act was adopted by the House of Representatives on September 29, by the Senate on October 4, and became law as Title II, Section 205(e) of the antipoverty law with the President's signature on November 8. Congress authorized $33 million for the Scheuer program, and on February 24, 1967, the Department of Labor, Manpower Administration, to which the program had been delegated, issued its first set of guidelines for the New Careers program. (We will use New Careers in capital letters to refer to this program and will use lower case for the general effort.) The language of the amendment made clear its purpose.

The Director is authorized to make grants or enter into agreements with any state or local agency or private organization to pay all or part of the costs of adult work training and employment programs for unemployed or low-income persons involving activities designed to improve the physical, social, economic, or cultural condition of the community or areas served in fields including, but not limited to health, education and welfare, neighborhood redevelopment, and public safety.

Four factors were to characterize the programs funded through the amendment: (a) development of entry-level employment opportunities, (b) assurance of maximum prospects for advancement and continued employment, (c) provision of a broad range of supportive services, and (d) inclusion of educational and training assistance.

In 1967, the Economic Opportunity Act was amended, and the Scheuer "New Careers" and Nelson "Operation Mainstream" programs separated. The

New Careers program was extended to include youth between sixteen and twenty-one, the phrases "new types of careers," "new methods of structuring jobs," "providing job-ladder opportunities," and "career advancement" were all added. Both committees of Congress which considered the Economic Opportunity Act gave special attention to the New Careers section. The House pointed to the need for more attention to the career-ladder concept and also expressed concern that permanent jobs be available at the end of the two-year period of federal subsidy.[20] The Senate echoed this concern for permanent jobs and added attention to the need "to break down traditional barriers, such as civil service regulations and professional 'standards.' "[21]

In 1969, the only major changes in the Economic Opportunity Act concerned New Careers and Operation Mainstream, which together were separated from other antipoverty manpower programs and given a special title in the law (Title I-E). In doubling the authorization requested by the President, the House Committee noted:

[these] two programs . . . have experienced an unusually high degree of success and usefulness; the demonstrated potential of hitherto excluded groups of people to make meaningful work contributions and to seek career advancement has been unquestionable.[22]

The Congress was particularly impressed:

The New Careers program's enrollment retention rate has been high, due, in part, to the opportunity to go beyond the entry level position to jobs with more responsibility and salaries.[23]

Based on their experience in providing technical assistance to 53 of the more than 100 New Careers projects, Jacob Fishman, President of the University Research Corporation, in an appearance before the House Antipoverty Subcommittee, reported the following:

There was a significant program-holding power, with a retention rate of 85 percent, and a dropout rate of 15 percent. Of the dropouts, 8 percent left for positive reasons, such as another job, and 7 percent left for negative reasons.

There was a sharp increase in income. Prior to enrollment, 61 percent were unemployed, 28 percent were on welfare, and the 11 percent employed had an average annual income of $2,100. While in the program, 60 percent had Level I jobs (average annual salary $3,880); 37 percent had Level II jobs (average annual salary $4,231); and 3 percent had Level III jobs (figures not available). There was also a wide distribution by service field; 34 percent, health (one third in mental health); 32 percent, education (over four fifths in the classroom); 13 percent, social services; 12 percent, law enforcement and corrections; and 9 percent, other. As to the participants themselves, 78 percent were Black, 80 percent were female, 48 percent had not completed high school, 38 percent were married, and their average age was twenty-nine.[24]

LEGISLATION AND THE PARAPROFESSIONAL

While the heartland of new careers was occupied by the successive versions of the Scheuer Amendment, legislation in various other fields was "new careerized."

The President, in his message on education and health, February 28, 1967, said: "New kinds of school personnel, such as teacher aides, are needed to help schools." He called for federal legislation to train aides as part of "a broader approach to training for the education professions." The Higher Education Act Amendments of 1967, which incorporated these ideas, were introduced by Congressman Carl Perkins and Senator Wayne Morse, and became Part D of the Higher Education Act of 1965, The Education Professions Development Act (PL 90-35). Programs to train aides were specifically mentioned in the law with both congressional committees stating that it "cannot overstate its interest in providing support for this type of program." Further, the bill encouraged the development of career-ladder programs for aides.[25] In addition to this new law, the Elementary and Secondary Education Act, the largest source of federal support for education, was amended to encourage the use of aides and to require, where aides were used, "coordinated programs of training in which education aides and the professional staff whom they are assisting will participate together."[26] The Vocational Education Act Amendments of 1968 included support for research and training for "new and emerging careers and occupations."[27]

As noted above, the 1961 juvenile delinquency legislation provided early support of paraprofessional projects. The Juvenile Delinquency Prevention and Control Act of 1968 (PL 90-445), an expanded version of the by-then lapsed 1961 law, included "special provision (Section 201) for the training of youths and adults for New Careers in fields related to juvenile delinquency and control."[28] And the Omnibus Crime Control and Safe Streets Act of 1968 (PL 90-351) provided for community service officers, local people who would work in police-community relations, community-patrol activities, and neighborhood participation in crime prevention.[29]

In health, where no single piece of legislation or even portion of a bill contains new careers language, such programs have been funded under the Allied Health Professions Training Act with its support for "training of new types of health technologists and technicians," and the Health Manpower Act's special-projects section call "to develop training for new levels or types of health-professions personnel."[30]

The broadly permissive language of the 1935 Social Security Act which allowed for the employment of some paraprofessionals was amended in 1967 to require that state plans provide for the following:

> the training and effective use of paid subprofessional staff, with particular emphasis on the full-time or part-time employment of recipients and other persons of low-income, as community service aides.[31]

For the first time, the employment of paraprofessionals was a mandatory part of a major grant-in-aid program and assured continuing budgetary and administrative support. In fiscal year 1970, there were 10,592 subprofessionals employed by local welfare agencies, most as eligibility technicians and homemakers. Although not required by the law, 15 states filled positions at both entry and subsequent levels and thus promoted a job-ladder concept for these workers.

The Vocational Rehabilitation Amendments of 1968 provided for a double use of new careers concepts as they "aim both at using nonprofessional New Careerists in rehabilitation services and at creating New Career job opportunities in public service for the handicapped served by rehabilitation agencies."[32] The Narcotic Addict Rehabilitation Act of 1968 provided for the training of new types of technical personnel, and the Drug Abuse Education Act of 1969 specified programs for "paraprofessional and community and neighborhood workers in new careers type occupations." The 1970 Amendments to the Mental Retardation Facilities and Community Mental Health Centers Construction Act of 1968 had provision for training and employment of paraprofessionals.

In 1970, the U.S. Department of Labor reallocated funds diverted from the Job Corps and Neighborhood Youth Corps and established the Public Service Careers Program (PSCP). Part C of PSCP continued, in a truncated form, the Scheuer Amendment New Careers program, while Parts A and B provided for grants for the training of paraprofessionals. Part D was for training of entry-level workers for and upgrading of those already employed by the federal government. A comparison of the New Careers model and PSCP shows that the Labor Department accepts the new-careers concepts of hire first, training and education built in; packaging of supportive services; decredentializing; and upgrading possibilities. What it does not include is job creation, mandated upgrading, role for community action agencies, and pressure for basic service system redesign.

New Careers	PSCP Plans A and B
Funds for salaries—job creation	No salary support or job creation
Funds for training and supportive services	Funds for training and supportive services
Requirements for upgrading of entry-level workers	Entry-level employment and/or upgrading but not required
Exclusion of present workers	Inclusion of present workers
Efforts to break credential barriers and restrictive agency practices	Efforts to break credential barriers and restrictive agency practices
Grants made through local anti-poverty agencies	Direct grants to state and local governments

The absence of job creation in the Labor Department's PSCP marks a sharp difference from the new careers advocates' concern for expanded public sector employment. In *New Careers for the Poor,* Pearl and Riessman had called for one million new jobs, a figure dwarfed by the five million public jobs called for by Americans for Democratic Action in 1966, and the 5.3 million jobs the National Commission on Technology Automation and Economic Progress said could be filled by persons with relatively low skills in order to meet presently unmet social needs.[33] In 1967, Senator Joseph Tydings and Abraham Ribicoff each introduced legislation for massive public service employment; similar bills were introduced in each successive year by these and other congressmen. In 1970, the Congress passed but the President vetoed the Manpower Act which included a $4.2 billion authorization for job creation. And, in 1971, thirty-four senators introduced the Emergency Employment Act which, at a 4.5 percent unemployment level, would provide $500 million for job creation and as much as $1 billion should unemployment reach 7 percent. The Black Caucus in the House of Representatives has proposed a million-person public service employment program.

THE CURRENT SITUATION

Some of the range of paraprofessional programs can be seen from the job titles of the East St. Louis Scheuer Amendment program, which include inhalation technician, laboratory technician, teacher aide, clinic technician, Girl Scout district adviser aide, home service consultant, production specialist, media technician, speed technician, audiovisual specialist, research aide, community worker, probation-officer aide, recreation leader, case aide, and social-work aide. But it is not only new jobs which new careers advocates seek.

Pearl and Riessman had set five goals for the new careers effort: (a) a sufficient number of jobs for all persons without work; (b) the jobs be so defined that placements exist for the unskilled and uneducated; (c) that the jobs be permanent and provide opportunities for careers; (d) that there be opportunities for advancement; and (e) that the work contribute to the well being of society.[34] Clearly these are goals far beyond the early and simple notion of relieving the professional of so-called nonprofessional chores. Indeed, the Vice-President of the College for Human Services, a college for paraprofessionals, formulated the new-careers program as going beyond helping professionals. Following is her list of five basic goals:

1. Different kinds of people should be able to enter the helping professions. . . .
2. Traditional routes to professionalism should be reevaluated. . . .
3. Experimentation and innovation in staffing patterns in the human services can give much needed new dimensions to the quality of the human service. . . .

4. "New professionals" should be trained and challenged to develop their individual potentials to make their own contribution to service. . . .

5. New Careers programs can contribute to the competence and resources of individuals and communities. . . .[35]

Another way of formulating the program's goals is to identify who may benefit from it. After surveying some fifteen programs in education which used auxiliaries, Garda W. Bowman and Gordon J. Klopf suggested possible benefits to the following: the pupil, the teacher, other professionals, the auxiliary, the school administrator, the auxiliaries' family life, and the community at large.[36]

James Farmer, as Assistant Secretary at the Department of Health, Education, and Welfare, was instrumental in establishing its Office of New Careers, and arrived at two basic goals of new careers (in health):

for the people of the ghettoes, barrios, and other areas of poverty . . . it can provide meaningful jobs and careers, not dead-end jobs or make work, but careers for which advancement is built in and not the privilege of a few. And, second, it can mean more and better health care for them, their families, and their community.[37]

Each of these statements of goals assumes a certain set of characteristics of program participants and activities. The paraprofessionals are formulation "indigenous" as opposed to "ubiquitous."[38] Something of the contrast between the older paraprofessional programs, the efforts of the early 1960's to find new manpower sources, and the new efforts can be portrayed in the mental-health field as follows:[39]

	Traditional Nonprofessionals	New Nonprofessionals	Indigenous Nonprofessionals
Ethnic Group	Black and Puerto Rican	White	Black and Puerto Rican
Class	Lower-Class	Middle- and Upper-Class	Lower-Class
Education	Nondegreed	Degreed	Nondegreed
Work Done	Primarily auxiliary	Substantive therapeutic	Substantive therapeutic
Indigeneity	Nonindigenous	Nonindigenous	Indigenous

Arthur Pearl and Frank Riessman early identified some of the reasons for the potential success of the so-called indigenous aide: Those who are poor, live in the neighborhood, and know the people and community, do not need to validate themselves. They describe his insider's know-how, savvy and working life style as direct, active, and partisan; his capacity to be an acceptable role model, a significant other; his ability to communicate between classes; and his satisfaction from community-serving work.[40] Research done in 1965 and 1966 on the first large-scale efforts at using indigenous aides (in the OEO's community action program), corroborated these assertions. One study described the aides as enthusiastic, hard working, seeing the work as more than a job, and the authors reported that hard-core aides were as effective as those "creamed" in selection.[41] Another reported:

> Aides are functioning well, frequently above anticipated levels. And it has become increasingly evident that competence is not necessarily a factor that stems from specific levels of formal education or previous work experience. [42]

And both studies, which together examined agencies employing some 10 percent of the paraprofessionals in Community Action Programs (CAP), found similar weaknesses. These included unwillingness of professionals to delegate meaningful jobs, too few men, inadequate training, reluctance of professionals to fire indigenous paraprofessionals, and primarily one-level jobs at salaries barely if at all above the poverty level.[43]

Some of these and similar program failures and concern for protection of the indigeneity of paraprofessionals led to various criticisms of the program. (Here we will only briefly note areas of criticism; the following chapters present a fuller discussion.) The general issue of social service programs versus social action and the related danger of cooptation of the paraprofessional was raised in several quarters.[44] Others were concerned with various facets of overidentification with professionals.[45]

Charles G. Grosser showed that indigenous paraprofessionals were significantly more accurate than professionals in assessing the community's views, he also found that one could not link accuracy of assessment with high performance in the actual work.[46] However, unlike the previously cited critics who appear to have accepted the strengths of the indigenous paraprofessional, Sherman Barr states:

> It is extremely difficult to vitiate the effects of the many years of poverty, brutalization, and discrimination endured by many poor indigenous persons. Expected limitations remain pervasive in spite of training efforts.
>   Those who were most successful had in the main experienced less poverty, were better educated, and had managed their lives with a reasonable degree of success and productivity.[47]

Barr further stated that "many professional workers" were not convinced that being poor, per se, enabled the indigenous worker to see problems differently or to perform better; that the paraprofessional's role as a "significant other" to the client population diminished as the agency itself gained credibility; that not all paraprofessionals had basic know-how; that "the distinctive attributes of indigenous nonprofessionals—if indeed they are distinctive at all—can be learned by more qualified nonprofessionals"; and, finally, that there are "extremely negative, judgmental, and punitive attitudes that many indigenous workers have toward other poor."[48]

While apparently he did not share Barr's fundamental questioning of the uniqueness and strength of the indigenous paraprofessional—indeed, his data give evidence at least as to uniqueness—Grosser did have a larger criticism than the question of work effectiveness, noted above. In the introduction of a book concerning paraprofessionals in social work and psychology, Grosser wrote:

> Use of nonprofessional personnel has been viewed as a device to accomplish professional reform; and even further, to relieve chronic unemployment, redistribute national resources, and integrate those who are excluded from the political and social processes of the nations.
> . . . the new careers movement, as this phenomenon has been designated, has, in our view, inflated a useful and relevant, albeit limited, strategy to the grandiose status of a social movement.[49]

To the charge of grandiosity there will be other answers on other occasions. It is interesting to note, however, that new careers has generated far more attention than is normally attracted to a "useful and relevant, albeit limited, strategy." Few if any topics have received the attention that has come to new careers across the entire spectrum of human-service works. One cannot read a volume of any major health, education, or social service journal since 1965 without finding some article or reference to new careers. (An incomplete bibliography of items relating to new careers up to 1969 includes over a thousand items.[50]) No part of the antipoverty program, except for the participation of the poor (of which new careers is itself a part), has had as much attention. And it appears that no feature of human service practice has had as broad reverberations in the various professions.

It is, however, a properly narrower topic that we will consider here. In reviewing the two studies of the early use of paraprofessionals in community-action programs, an observer noted that neither had "been primarily concerned with the quality of professional services."[51] It is to this topic that we will address two basic questions. First, what does the paraprofessional do? And second, to what effect does it relate to the client, patient, student, in short, the service consumer?

In subsequent chapters, we will consider the fields of education, mental health, social work, health, and police and corrections. The last chapter assesses the state of the art, presents a summary of current issues and problems, and briefly touches on some of the ramifications of these programs which go beyond the specific topic of the paraprofessional and his performance.

The evaluation of human service practice, particularly as to how it affects the consumer, is highly problematic. One must first achieve clarity as to the objectives of the effort and then provide instruments of measurement. Neither part of the endeavor has been well achieved in any human service field. An additional complication is the effort to disentangle from the variety of factors which impinge on the patient, client, student, and so forth the effect of a particular factor, in our case, that of the paraprofessional. Thus, we find ourselves in a situation where no single study is adequate in itself. Surely no single study can offer conclusive evidence by itself, although, as we will see, a number do offer powerful evidence.

In particular, the reader will want to take note of the Minneapolis study in education, along with the Indiana, Kentucky, and Florida programs; the work of Robert B. Ellsworth, Charles B. Truax, and Francine Sobey in mental health; the Alameda County, California, Mobilization for Youth (New York City), and Project Enable experience in social work; in health, the reports on the programs of the New York City municipal hospitals, the Denver comprehensive health center, the Los Angeles nutrition program, family planning outreach, and the Contra Costa immunization program; and in corrections, the Manhattan Court Employment Project (MCEP), Project Crossroads in Washington, D.C., and the Los Angeles Reeducation of Delinquency Through Expansion of Opportunity (RODEO) program.

Finally, the point is that the multiplicity of evidence derived from a great variety of sources, stemming from different investigator perspectives, using diverse methods and indices, leads to the conclusion that paraprofessionals play an important role as service agents and contribute to the well being of human service agency consumers in highly significant and often unique ways.

NOTES

1. Robert M. Vidaver, "The Mental Health Technician: Maryland's Design for a New Health Career," *American Journal of Psychiatry*, CXXV, 8 (February, 1969), 1013; Solomon Kobrin, "The Chicago Area Project: A Twenty-Five Year Assessment," *Annals of the American Academy of Political and Social Science*, CCCXLI (March, 1959), 19-29.

2. Barry Greenberg, "Review of Literature Relating to the Use of Nonprofessionals in Education (From 1942 to 1967)" (New York: New Careers Development Center, New York University, 1967), p. 1; Garda W. Bowman and Gordon J. Klopf, *New Careers and Roles in the American School: A Study of Auxiliary Personnel in Education* (New York: Bank Street College of Education, 1968), p. 6.

3. Greenberg, *loc. cit.*

4. *Ibid.*, pp. 2-3; Bowman and Klopf, *op. cit.*, p. 7; James Donald Sarwin, "Criteria for Statutory Provisions for the Employment of Teacher Aides in Public School Districts" (unpublished Ph.D. dissertation, University of Colorado, 1969), p. 21; Charles B. Park, "The Bay City Experiment . . . As Seen by the Director," *Journal of Teacher Education*, VII, 2 (June, 1956), 101-10; "A Symposium: The Bay City, Michigan Experiment, A Cooperative Study for The Better Utilization of Teacher Competencies," *Journal of Teacher*

Education, VII, 2 (June, 1956), 110-52; D. Richard Wynn and Richard W. DeRemer, "Staff Utilization, Development, and Evaluation," *Review of Educational Research*, XXXI, 4 (October, 1961), 393-405; *Decade of Experiment: The Fund for the Advancement of Education, 1951-61* (New York: Ford Foundation, 1961).

5. Marcella Farrar and Mary L. Hemmy, "Use of Nonprofessional Staff in Work With the Aged," *Social Work*, VIII, 3 (July, 1963), 44; Verne Weed and William H. Denham, "Toward More Effective Use of The Nonprofessional Worker: A Recent Experiment," *Social Work*, VI, 4 (October, 1961), 29-36.

6. Vidaver, *loc. cit.*

7. Aaron Schmais, *Implementing Nonprofessional Programs in Human Services* (New York: Graduate School of Social Work, New York University, 1967), p. 7; Wilbur Hoff, "Role of the Community Health Aide in Public Health Programs," *Public Health Reports*, LXXXIV, 11 (November, 1969), 999.

8. Henry Saltzman, "The Poor and the Schools," in Arthur Pearl and Frank Riessman, *New Careers for the Poor: The Nonprofessional in Public Service* (New York: Free Press, 1965), pp. 49-50; Schmais, *loc. cit.*, Hoff, *loc. cit.*

9. Farrar and Hemmy, *op. cit.*, pp. 44-47; Margaret J. Rioch *et al.*, "National Institute of Mental Health Pilot Study in Training Mental Health Counselors," *American Journal of Orthopsychiatry*, XXXIII, 4 (July, 1963), 678-89; Laura Epstein, "Differential Use of Staff: A Method to Expand Social Services," *Social Work*, VII, 4 (October, 1962), 66-72; Jules D. Holzberg and Robert H. Knapp, "The Social Interaction of College Students and Chronically Ill Mental Patients" (paper presented at the American Orthopsychiatric Association Conference, Chicago, 1964); Sol Mitchen *et al.*, "A Community Educational Program for the Emotionally Disturbed Child," *American Journal of Orthopsychiatry*, XXXIV, 4 (July, 1964), 705-13.

10. George Brager, "The Indigenous Worker: A New Approach for the Social Work Technician," *Social Work*, X, 2 (April, 1965), 33-40.

11. J. L. Massimo and M. F. Shore, "Effectiveness of a Comprehensive Vocationally Oriented Therapeutic Program for Adolescent Boys," *American Journal of Orthopsychiatry*, XXXIII, 6 (June, 1963), 634-42.

12. Richard A. Cloward and Lloyd E. Ohlin, *Opportunity and Delinquency: A Theory of Delinquent Gangs* (Glencoe, Ill.: The Free Press, 1960).

13. Frank Riessman, "The Revolution in Social Work: The New Nonprofessional" (New York: Mobilization for Youth, 1963).

14. Beryce W. MacLennan and William L. Klein, "Utilization of Groups in Job Training for the Socially Deprived," *International Journal of Group Psychology*, XV, 4 (October, 1965), 424-33; Beryce W. MacLennan, "New Careers as Human Service Aides," *Children*, XIII, 5 (September-October, 1966), 190-94.

15. Robert Reiff and Frank Riessman, *The Indigenous Nonprofessional: A Strategy of Change in Community Action and Community Mental Health Programs* (New York: National Institute of Labor Education, 1964).

16. J. Douglas Grant, "The Offender as a Correctional Manpower Resource," in Pearl and Riessman, *op. cit.*, pp. 226-34; Schmais, *op. cit.*, 8-12.

17. Schmais, *op. cit.*, p. 6.

18. Frank Riessman, "Memorandum to Representative James Scheuer," March 7, 1966.

19. R. A. Nixon, *Legislative Dimensions of the New Careers Program: 1970* (New York: Center for the Study of the Unemployed, New York University, 1970). Much of the following discussion of the legislative history of new careers is based on Nixon's definitive text.

20. U.S. Congress, House of Representatives, Report No. 866, Committee on Education and Labor, *Economic Opportunity Amendments of 1967*, October 27, 1967, pp. 17-18.

21. U.S. Congress, Senate Report No. 563, Committee on Labor and Public Welfare, *Economic Opportunity Amendments of 1967*, September 12, 1967, p. 25.

22. U.S. Congress, House of Representatives Report No. 91-684, *Economic Opportunity Act Amendments of 1969*.

23. *Ibid*.

24. National Institute for New Careers, *An Assessment of Technical Assistance and Training Needs in New Careers Projects Being Sponsored by the United States Training and Employment Service, Manpower Administration, U.S. Department of Labor* (Washington, D.C.: University Research Corporation, 1969).

25. Nixon, *op. cit.*, pp. 15-16.

26. *Ibid.*, Title V, Sec. 144, and Title II, Sec. 205(a), respectively, p. 18.

27. *Ibid.*, p. 19.

28. *Ibid.*, p. 22.

29. *Ibid.*, Title I, Part C, Sec. 301, p. 21.

30. *Ibid.*, p. 24.

31. *Ibid.*, p. 26.

32. *Ibid.*, p. 25. See also Special Edition, *New Careers Newsletter*, II, 4 (Fall, 1968), "Voc Rehab—A Partner in New Careers."

33. National Commission on Technology, Automation and Economic Progress, *Technology and the American Economy* (Vol. 1; Washington, D.C., 1966).

34. Pearl and Riessman, *op. cit.*, p. 2.

35. Laura Pires Houston, "Black People, New Careers and Humane Human Services," *Social Casework*, LI, 5 (May, 1970), 292.

36. Bowman and Klopf, *op. cit.*, p. 5.

37. James Farmer, "Demand for Health Services Creates Medical Manpower Crisis," *Afro-American Newspaper*, September, 1969, p. 90.

38. Reiff and Riessman, *loc. cit.*

39. Rioch, *loc. cit.*, for information on the new professionals; Frank Riessman and Emanuel Hallowitz, "Neighborhood Service Center Program," a report to the U.S. Office of Economic Opportunity on the South Bronx Neighborhood Service Center, December, 1965, for information on the indigenous nonprofessionals.

40. Pearl and Riessman, *op. cit.*, pp. 85-87.

41. Daniel Yankelovich, Inc., *A Study of the Nonprofessional in the CAP* (New York, 1966).

42. Edith F. Lynton, "The Nonprofessional Scene," *American Child*, XLIX, 1 (Winter, 1967), 12.

43. *Ibid.*, Yankelovich, *loc. cit.*

44. Paul A. Kurzman, "The New Careers Movement and Social Change," *Social Casework*, LI, 1 (January, 1970), 22-27; Margaret A. Thompson, "Contamination of New Careerists by Professionalization: Fact or Fancy?" (Minneapolis: New Careers Research, University of Minnesota, 1969); Pearl and Riessman, *loc. cit.*; Reiff and Riessman, *loc. cit.*

45. Kurzman, *op. cit.*, p. 26; Perry Levinson and Jeffrey Schiller, "Role Analysis of the Indigenous Nonprofessional," *Social Work*, XI, 3 (July, 1966), 99; Charles G. Grosser, "Local Residents as Mediators Between Middle-Class Professional Workers and Lower-Class Clients," *Social Service Review*, XL, 1 (March, 1966), 56-63; Pauline Coggs and Vivian R. Robinson, "Training Indigenous Community Leaders for Employment in Social Work," *Social Casework*, XLVIII, 5 (May, 1967), 281.

46. Charles G. Grosser, "Class Orientation of the Indigenous Staff," in George Brager and Francis P. Purcell, eds., *Community Action Against Poverty* (New Haven: College and University Press, 1967).

47. Sherman Barr, *Some Observations on the Practice of Nonprofessional Workers* (New York: Mobilization for Youth, 1966), pp. 12-13.

48. *Ibid.*; Sherman Barr, "A Professional Takes a Second Look," *American Child*, XLIX, 1 (Winter, 1967), 14-17.

49. Charles G. Grosser *et al.*, eds., *Nonprofessionals in the Human Services* (San Francisco: Jossey-Bass, Inc., 1969), 6.

50. National Institute for New Careers, *New Careers Bibliography: Paraprofessionals in the Human Services* (Washington, D.C.: University Research Corporation, 1970).

51. Gertrude S. Goldberg, "Nonprofessionals in Human Services," in Grosser *et al.*, *op. cit.*, p. 25.

2

EDUCATION

With his characteristic sharpness, Arthur Pearl distinguished three types of staffing patterns. First, there is the plantation system, in which paraprofessionals are seen as a permanent proletariat lacking any advancement opportunities. Second, there is the medical system, in which there is a sharp distinction of roles, and while there may be upgrading within the role (licensed practical nurse or LPN to senior LPN, for example), there is no leap from role to role (registered nurse or RN to doctor). And third, there is a new careers design, in which education that is built into the job is seen as a continuous link between various levels of work.[1]

The earliest use of paraprofessionals in U.S. schools, Lancaster's monitorial system (1798), surely fits Pearl's plantation-system model. There, as an economy measure, young men were used to multiply the number of persons an adult teacher could teach. The monitor acted as little more than a transmission belt from teacher to pupils. An unplanned for and serendipitous effect was that the monitors themselves learned by teaching.[2] The monitorial system died out in the 1830's, partly due to an excess of greed and partly because in the post-Civil War period great emphasis was placed on certificated teachers.

THE BAY CITY PROJECT

The Bay City, Michigan, project fits Pearl's medical-system model. A grant was made to Central Michigan State College of Education to support a joint project of the college and the Bay City school system. A study showed that "teachers were spending anywhere from 21 to 69 percent of their time on nonteaching chores."[3] Faced with rising enrollment, the project sought to develop more effective ways to utilize staff. Eight college-trained women were employed as teacher aides. A final evaluation by the college found that teachers with aides spent more time on instructional activities; there was little objective evidence bearing on the quality of instruction in classrooms with teacher aides as opposed to those without; teacher aides facilitated better deployment of teachers and experimentation with staffing, although there was no noticeable change in teaching methods; the program had little effect on over-all costs; and many of the aides were potential recruits for teaching (in fact, five of the initial eight went on to become teachers).[4] The project's director listed these positive and specific findings:

> One hundred percent of the parents interviewed felt that their children enjoyed school more under the aide plan. . . . Eighty-three percent felt that their children learned more, and 17 percent felt they learned as much.
> Teachers working with aides indicated that under the aide program they found more time for work with individual children and small groups. They had more time for instructional preparation, and more time for recitation, pupil discussion [and other] kinds of activities.[5]

The program was adopted by more than 50 other Michigan systems. Fairfield, Connecticut, and New York City developed volunteer- and paid-aide programs. By 1961, there were over 5,000 aides across the country. In 1956, the Education Testing Service (ETS) conducted a lay-reader experiment in New Jersey and Massachusetts, and this offshoot of the Bay City program had spread to some 120 school systems by 1961.[6]

In a summary of its efforts in this area, the Ford Foundation, which provided support to Bay City and many successive efforts, wrote the following:

> The significance of the Bay City type of project is that aides are used to improve *the quality of education* by freeing teachers to spend their time in actual teaching. This use of aides was a distinct departure from the past, particularly from the monitorial system that flourished in the U.S. a century or more ago, in which aides were used to educate large numbers of children inexpensively—and inadequately.[7]

But the general consensus was less optimistic than the sponsors; it focused on the fact that aides were not replacements for teachers and that the use of aides could not be a justification for larger classes.[8] For many in the increasingly organized teaching profession, Bay City came to be remembered as an effort to hire "cheap teachers." A survey of articles in the professional education journals between 1942 and 1957 found critics of aide programs charging that aides were used to justify larger classes, that not all teachers could work with aides, that evaluation was difficult, and that use of aides encouraged rote learning. Advocates claimed that aides were a valuable, temporary measure, that the classroom was enriched by the use of another adult, and that the aide was a possible teacher recruit.[9]

J. L. Trump, in his comprehensive examination of secondary education, enumerated six categories of teacher functions: professional teacher, paraprofessional assistant, clerk, general aide, community consultant, and staff specialist.[10] This proposal, important as much for Trump's position in the education establishment as for the merit of the ideas, is the fullest expression of what Pearl labeled the medical-system model, that is, sharp role differentiation with no mobility from role to role. Nearly a decade later, quite similar notions which suffer from many of the same faults as Trump's design were put forth regarding "staff differentiation," primarily by Dwight Allen, based on work at the Temple City, California school.

Many of Trump's ideas came to be incorporated in the work of the Committee on the Experimental Study of the Staff in the Secondary School. A 1962 study of the secondary schools involved found most aides were teachers in training; others were college students, college-trained adults, and least of all, other adults. The major functions they performed were as lay readers, clerks, objective-test graders, library assistants, and study-hall supervisors.[11] At all grade levels, a 1953 survey of 800 New York school districts found that 51 percent used paraprofessionals (a total of 2,389), with "exceedingly favorable results."[12]

In a summary of the situation shortly before the new thrust of the antipoverty effort, Robert Anderson wrote:

> Only a decade ago, when pilot projects in the use of teacher aides and other nonprofessional assistants first began to appear in the literature, the predominate reaction of the profession was negative, even hostile. In 1964, it is rare to find discussions of utilization of school personnel in which nonprofessionals are not considered a welcome addition.[13]

THE SURGE OF AIDES

The implementation of the Elementary and Secondary Education Act, along with the Economic Opportunity Act, led to a rapid increase in the use of paraprofessionals. A 1966 survey found that 2 percent of the programs then operating had begun in the period 1930-49; 17 percent in 1950-59; 36 percent in 1960-64, and 45 percent in 1965-66.[14] Three national studies by the National Education Association's (NEA) Research Division and smaller surveys in Indiana and California, although not of comparable universe, showed the changes in paraprofessional employment from 1965-66 to 1968-69.[15] Trends over this period appeared to include an increased use of paraprofessionals, a higher percentage of paid paraprofessionals, a stable concentration in the elementary grades, and a slight shift to more instructional activity.

The annual report of the Commissioner of Education on the state of the education profession showed the concentration of paraprofessional programs in poverty-neighborhood schools.[16] As Table 2 indicates, large city elementary

TABLE 1

School-District Use of Paraprofessionals, 1965-69

	1965-66	1966-67	1966-67	1967-68	1968-69
Number of School Districts surveyed	251[a]	63[b]	1,204[c]	1,153[d]	1,199[d]
Number using paraprofessionals	217	49	416	743	799
Number of paraprofessionals	29,995	334		29,938	40,295
Percent paid	67		98	82	84
Level paraprofessional used (percent)					
Preschool and kindergarten	21	⎫	15	10	13
Grades 1-3	17	⎬ 74	25	⎫ 62	⎫ 62
Grades 4-6	29	⎭	15	⎭	⎭
Junior high school	16	⎫ 26	⎫ 45	11	10
Senior high school	16	⎭	⎭	17	15
Funding source (percent)					
Federal only	25	81	–	–	30
State and local	25	16	–	–	18
Both	50	–	–	–	52
Paraprofessionals per teacher	–	–	–	0.19	0.26
Rank order of paraprofessional activities					
Secretarial	1	1	1	–	1
Classroom housekeeper	2	–	–	–	–
Setting up audiovisual equipment	3	–	–	–	–
Helping with clothing	4	2	–	–	–
Supervising playground	5	–	–	–	4
Correcting tests/homework	6	–	2	–	3
Lunchroom assistance	–	3	3	–	2
Small group instruction	–	4	5	–	5
Individual instruction	–	–	4	–	6

[a]Districts with 12,000 or more pupils, nationwide.
[b]Indiana School Corporations.
[c]California School districts.
[d]Districts with 6,000 or more pupils, nationwide, excluding New York City.

Sources: "Teacher Aides in Public Schools," *National Education Association Research Bulletin,* XLVI, 6 (May, 1967), 30-33, as well as XLVIII, 1 (March, 1970), 11-12; *Teacher Aides: A Status Report* (Terre Haute: School of Education, Indiana State University, 1968); and California Teachers Association, *Teacher Aides in California Schools and School Districts, 1966-1967,* "Research Bulletin," No. 206 (Burlingame, 1967).

schools in poverty areas were most likely to have classroom aides (62%), while large city, nonpoverty, secondary schools were least likely to have them (15%). Again, Table 3 shows that aides were more concentrated in poverty schools and in the elementary grades.

A number of state and local studies mirror the national pattern. In Wayne County, Michigan, the paraprofessional to teacher ratio was about 1 to 4.5, and paraprofessionals were assigned to twenty-six different job titles.[17] A 1964 report on Illinois programs took a very cool tone toward paraprofessionals in instructional activities.[18] However, by 1967, the state had enacted legislation specifically authorizing local boards of education to employ noncertificated personnel.[19]

TABLE 2

Schools Without Classroom Aides, by percent

	Poverty		Nonpoverty	
	Elementary	Secondary	Elementary	Secondary
All	42	64	65	72
Large cities	28	74	63	95

Source: *The Education Professions, An Annual Report on the People Who Serve Our Schools and Colleges, 1969-70* (Washington, D.C.: Office of Education, U.S. Department of Health, Education, and Welfare, 1970), Table 14.

TABLE 3

Additional New Staff Needed as Percent of Current Staff

	Poverty		Nonpoverty	
	Elementary	Secondary	Elementary	Secondary
Total Staff Needed	49	44	39	33
Classroom Aides	15	12	10	8
School Aides	137	706	938	1,010

Source: *The Education Professions, An Annual Report on the People Who Serve Our Schools and Colleges, 1969-70* (Washington, D.C.: Office of Education, U.S. Department of Health, Education and Welfare, 1970), Table 15.

An NEA survey in 1968 found that over 90 percent of teachers who had paraprofessionals "indicated that having an aide was helpful, and more than half said it was of *great* assistance." As to the work the paraprofessionals should do, 73 percent of the total sample of teachers surveyed favored paraprofessionals assisting with clerical duties but were less supportive of paraprofessionals giving assistance with certain types of classroom instruction (44%).[20] This range was mirrored in a 1967 survey of teachers in the Racine and Madison, Wisconsin, school systems who had paraprofessionals. There, 72 percent favored their use for relieving teachers of routine and clerical tasks, but only 34 percent favored properly trained paraprofessionals performing limited instructional tasks.[21]

PARAPROFESSIONALS AND PUPIL PERFORMANCE

Any effort to evaluate pupil performance is complicated, and the complications are increased immeasurably when one seeks to isolate the effect of a particular factor, such as the role of paraprofessionals, on that performance. Studies of performance are complicated by questions of what criterion is to be used, such as reading scores and the like, or more subtle measures in the cognitive area, to say nothing of the affective domain. As to identifying the effect of particular inputs, the chairman of a study group assessing the impact of teacher performance (the most studied variable), on pupil performance stated: *"At the present moment we cannot make any sort of meaningful quantitative estimate of the effect of teachers on student achievement."*[22] Thus, to assess the role of the paraprofessional on pupil learning, we must seek a variety of methods and sources, and, even so, express results with some caution. The data which follow were collected from many sources, came to the issues from different vantage points, and sought answers to varying questions. We believe that together they do what no single study does or can do, that is, make a persuasive, although assuredly not final, argument that paraprofessionals through their direct impact on students positively effect their learning. And, beyond this indication of direct effect on the pupil, there is data as to effect on teachers—changes in the allocation and use of their time and their behavior which allow for greater attention by the teacher to pupils.

The American Institute for Research on behalf of the Office of Education, conducted a survey of the professional educational literature, 1963-68, that described compensatory education programs.[23] Of the 1,000 programs described, 23 were found to have yielded "measured educational benefits of cognitive achievement." Of these 23, 10, or 43 percent, involved the use of paraprofessionals. As indicated above, there were relatively few paraprofessional programs before 1965, and, with the lag in reporting on concluded programs, there were few summaries in the literature before 1967. It is therefore unlikely that anywhere near 43 percent of the total sample of 1,000 programs used paraprofessionals.

The most carefully studied paraprofessional program in education to date is that of the Minneapolis Public Schools.[24] Between 1966 and 1968, that system employed between 225 and 300 paraprofessionals. In the spring of 1967, a survey of 231 paraprofessionals found that 54 percent were in the elementary grades, 94 percent were female, and they had a median age of 37.5.[25] In these characteristics, the paraprofessionals in this school system were similar to those across the nation. In order to test the effectiveness of paraprofessional performance on pupil learning, a study was conducted during early 1968. Nine kindergarten classes, each with about thirty pupils, half of whom were Black, were selected. Three classes had no aides, three had one aide, and three had five aides. All classes were given the Metropolitan Reading Readiness Test, Form R, in January and then again in May. The results, showing unweighted means, pretest, posttest, and gains are shown in Table 4.

TABLE 4

Pupil Performance Related to Number of Aides, Minneapolis, 1968

	0 Aides (n = 75)	1 Aide (n = 79)	5 Aides (n = 80)
Reading Readiness			
Pretest	41.8	38.2	40.7
Posttest	47.4	47.8	48.8
Gain	5.6	9.6	8.1
Number Readiness			
Pretest	8.2	8.1	8.4
Posttest	11.6	12.1	12.7
Gain	3.4	4.0	4.3
Total Readiness			
Pretest	53.5	49.7	52.8
Posttest	63.9	64.9	66.6
Gain	10.4	15.2	13.8

Source: William S. Bennett, Jr. and R. Frank Falk, *New Careers and Urban Schools* (New York: Holt, Rinehart, and Winston, 1970), p. 125.

Those classes with one aide made a 50 percent greater total gain than did those with no aide, or in terms of percentage gain over pretest, those with one aide gained 30 percent as compared with a 19 percent gain for those with no aide. On both total gain and percentage gain over pretest, those classes with five aides did better than those with no aide but not as well as those with one aide. The authors suggested that a reason for the lesser gain of those with five aides as compared to those with one might lie in the management problems presented with such a large number of adults in the classroom.[26]

A study of paraprofessional programs in rural Kentucky compared classes with paraprofessionals present in the classroom for different numbers of hours per day.[27] Paraprofessionals in the Model School, which had 235 children, worked 4 hours per day; those in 5 other schools, with a total of 1,061 children, worked 1.5 hours per day. While the desire of pupils to ask questions was about the same in the two sets of schools, the children in the Model School felt they could ask more questions. Also, paraprofessionals gave opportunity for more activities enjoyed by the children.[28]

Two smaller studies also suggested paraprofessional effects on pupil performance. In a Palo Alto, California, preschool program, the use of paraprofessionals led to pupils' improved verbal proficiency, more small-group activity, more child-to-child interaction, and more attention paid to children's language development.[29] And in Atlanta, Georgia, where 108 paraprofessionals worked in 47 poverty-neighborhood schools, it was found that reading gains of third-grade pupils were greatest in those Title I, Elementary and Secondary Education Act (ESEA), classes which used paraprofessionals as compared both with such schools which did not use them and with non-Title I schools.[30]

While the foregoing programs considered only the paraprofessionals' indigeneity as a special qualification, an Arlington, Massachusetts, program was concerned with the special effect of males on elementary-age children. Project Male, begun in 1967, involved part-time volunteers in kindergarten through third grade in three elementary schools; during the first 3 years of the project, 1,012 children were served. The project took as its starting point the fact that some 80 percent to 90 percent of all primary children who had social or academic difficulty were boys.[31] It was found, on test of psychological development as well as academic achievement, that boys who were in male-aided classes did better than those in female-aided classes or those with no paraprofessionals.

> Significantly greater improvement in scores from fall to spring on the Evanston Drawing Test of Emotional and Academic Achievement was found for 247 kindergarten boys in male-aided classes than for boys in control groups. Improvement was also greater for girls in the male-aided classes, although not as great as for boys.
>
> More significant and positive attitudes toward school and work activities were found in boys who were in male-aided classes as opposed to those in female- or nonaided classes.
>
> The number of boys performing at or above grade level was significantly greater in male-aided classes than in the female- or nonaided classes. The degree of this improvement increased in the second and third year of the program.[32]

The studies discussed above described paraprofessionals working as generalists in the classroom. The following three studies reported on them performing specialized tasks. The middle schools of Hammond, Indiana, used paraprofessionals in a corrective reading program. Between 1967 and 1970, they conducted "a study in the use of paraprofessional personnel in intensive corrective reading instruction."[33] The referral criteria for pupils to the program was an IQ of 90 or above and a reading level at least a year below grade. In fact, for the 832 pupils in the program over the three years, IQ ranged from 75 to 126, and students were from one to five years below grade in reading. About 60 percent of the pupils were boys, 25 percent from disadvantaged families, and they were about equally divided among the sixth, seventh, and eighth grades.

There were 22 paraprofessionals, 10 of whom had children with academic difficulties. The children received approximately an hour per week of instruction from the paraprofessionals. The performance of the children helped by the paraprofessionals was compared with a matched control group. Table 5 presents the gains over a school term of the experimental (with paraprofessionals) and control (without paraprofessionals) pupils; a weighted reading score developed by the program is used. The project director summarized the data presented in Table 5, as follows:

TABLE 5

Pupil Performance in a Tutoring Program, 1967-70

	Gain	Difference	Gain Above Normal
Grade 6			
Experimental	+14	+4	+4
Control	+10		
Grade 7			
Experimental	+12	+5	+2
Control	+ 7		
Grade 8			
Experimental	+18	+6	+8
Control	+12		

Source: Utilization of Paraprofessional Personnel in Intensive Remedial Reading, End of Project Report (Hammond, Ind.: City of Hammond Schools, 1970), p. 47.

On the basis of the comparison of experimental and control subjects and average growth scores with the norm of expectation, it can be stated that paraprofessionals can be used effectively in providing remedial reading instruction at the middle school level.[34]

Much this same model was used in some fifty other communities in twelve Middle-West states. The paraprofessionals were given twenty-one hours of programed instruction in tutoring, and they worked with the children about an hour a week. A significantly greater proportion of the tutored children progressed normally, that is, advanced from the second grade to third grade, than did those in the control group (59% and 41%, respectively). And those receiving tutoring were 59 percent less likely to need to be assigned to a special education class than were those in the control group.[35]

A tutorial program for children with serious reading retardation showed gains for both the children and their paraprofessional tutors. In that program, 15 paraprofessionals worked in 4 Brooklyn ghetto schools. They tutored 105 children two to four times a week. Three of the paraprofessionals had no high school diploma, and as a group, their reading level ranged from third to twelfth grade.

Final evaluation of the program showed behavioral and reading improvement among most of the 105 children. Tutors gained in reading level, in insight into the school as a social system, in sensitivity in child development and management and in teaching methodology.[36]

The three reports above described the effects of paraprofessionals in programs for students who were not doing well in school. In another report, the Fennville, Michigan, project found that paraprofessionals had greater effect on the more gifted students. First, they had found that the use of paraprofessionals in the homemaking curriculum had been successful:

> as measured by student opinion, teacher aide evaluations, parent and community thinking, judgments by consultants and administrators. [Therefore,] an experiment was designed and executed to measure the effect of the teacher aide on the behavior of students in the classroom."[37]

Two groups of ninth-grade girls were divided in order to obtain equal groups based on scores from the California Test of Mental Maturity. At the end of the year, the two classes were compared as to marks, test scores, days absent, and request for more advanced courses the next year. Based on these criteria, "students with greater intelligence accomplished more by the addition of trained aide staff per class, whereas the average and less able are not affected as markedly."[38]

Each of the reports cited above involved paraprofessionals working directly with students. The following two studies, one in Florida and the other in New York City, involved indigenous paraprofessionals who trained poverty-family mothers; they in turn worked with their own children. Fifteen "disadvantaged" women worked with nearly 300 mothers and their children in a program at the College of Education, University of Florida. The "parent educators" instructed the mothers in a series of exercises designed to provide physical, intellectual, and social stimulation for children from the age of three months through two years. As measured by the Griffiths Mental Development Scale, the children whose mothers were trained by the paraprofessionals did better on all scales—locomotor, personal-social, hearing and speech, eye and hand, and general performance—than did those in a matched control group whose parents did not receive this training. And a New York City program, Supplementary Teaching in Advanced Reading (STAR), used paraprofessionals to train parents to read to their children. Studies done on the youngsters, first-grade pupils from predominantly Puerto Rican families whose teachers identified them as likely reading failures, found that the children whose parents were trained by paraprofessionals one hour per week to read to them scored higher in nine different reading tests than did matched children who received two hours of remediation from professionals or a control group.[39]

As with the STAR program, reading was the criterion in an OEO-sponsored study of the Adult Basic Education program (ABE). So, too, the performance of paraprofessionals was compared to that of professionals. The purpose of the study was to find the most effective ABE system, and the findings on teacher performance were an incidental byproduct of the main study. It was found, regardless of the ABE system used, that the indigenous paraprofessionals (high school graduates or less) were more effective in terms of participant reading scores than either a certified remedial education teacher or a college graduate.[40]

A Georgia Head Start program compared language performance of pupils in a class that had both a teacher and a paraprofessional with those who had a paraprofessional alone. The Illinois Test of Psycholinguistic Abilities was used in a pre- and posttest study comparing two classes of each staffing design.

> It was found that during a four month Head Start program the children's performance on a linguistic test increased significantly regardless of the training level of the teacher. High school educated teachers, paraprofessionals, did just as well as college educated teachers in teaching children as determined by measurements of the children's language behavior.[41]

PARAPROFESSIONALS AND TEACHERS

While the impact of paraprofessionals would appear to be greatest in their direct effect on pupils, particularly given the special qualities of the indigenous worker, their role in freeing the teachers' time is important to consider in that it is what most paraprofessionals are employed to do, and for the effect they have on the teachers' activities. Another way to look at teacher time is suggested by a New York City study which reports that each secondary school uses a total of four full-time positions for nonteaching assignments at a cost of $8 million a year.[42]

The Minneapolis study described earlier asked teachers how much paraprofessionals freed them to do planning and preparation and to work directly with pupils. To the question on time for planning and preparation, the teachers' responses ranged from zero to thirty hours per week, with a median of fourteen hours per week. As to time saved for working directly with pupils, the answers ranged from zero to twenty hours, with a median of three hours.[43] Thus, combining the two medians, the use of paraprofessionals in the Minneapolis project saved teachers approximately seventeen hours a week. Similar findings have been reported from numerous programs. For example, a study of Wisconsin programs reported that 86 percent of the teachers with paraprofessionals were able to devote significantly more time to individual pupils as a result of their presence, and 88 percent of the teachers felt that the climate for learning had been significantly improved through the services of a paraprofessional.[44]

A study on the North Carolina Comprehensive School Improvement Project first noted the time saved for teachers as a result of the paraprofessionals' work and went on to state the following:

> Teacher time is increasingly redirected toward the central goal of instructional improvement in that (a) more time is spent in giving pupils individual and small group attention; (b) more time is devoted

to cooperative planning of learning opportunities for pupils; and (c) more attention is devoted to the pupil's personal-social needs.[45]

Furthermore, not only does the presence of a paraprofessional lead to the teacher having more time in the classroom to devote to both pupils and preparation while in class, but it also leads to more preparation at home. It seems that the role of the paraprofessional as another adult in the classroom encourages the teacher to this greater preparation.[46]

Based on their study of fifteen paraprofessional programs, a Bank Street College of Education team said that the introduction of the paraprofessional served as a catalytic force in the development of new roles for all the parties in the school system. They found that participating teachers perceived new roles for themselves which included a higher level of professionalism with emphasis on diagnosis, planning, and coordination. Teachers themselves saw this new role as additive rather than substitutive for teacher-pupil interaction.[47]

Some of the benefits to pupil, paraprofessional (their term is "auxiliary"), teacher, school, and community is described in an earlier Bank Street College report.

1. *To the pupil,* by providing more individualized attention by concerned adults, more mobility in the classroom, and more opportunity for innovation;

2. *To the teacher,* by rendering his role more satisfying in terms of status, and more manageable in terms of teaching conditions;

3. *To the other professionals,* by increasing the scope and effectiveness of their activities;

4. *To the auxiliary,* by providing meaningful employment which contributes at one and the same time to his development and to needs of society;

5. *To the school administrator,* by providing some answers to his dilemma of ever increasing needs for school services, coupled with a shortage of professionals to meet these needs—*a* solution, not *the* solution, and certainly not a panacea;

6. *To family life,* by giving auxiliaries, many of whom may someday become parents, the opportunity to learn child development principles in a reality situation;

7. *To the community at large,* by providing a means through which unemployed and educationally disadvantaged persons may enter the mainstream of productivity.[48]

A study conducted by the First National City Bank sought to measure the importance of various factors as they affected reading scores. They studied fifth-grade reading scores in the city's 557 elementary schools in 1968. In rank order, they found the following:

significant improvements in reading skills were associated with a principal's belief that he had a competent professional staff in the fourth and fifth grades, respected his teachers' aides working in the classroom and used them extensively, had meaningful parent and community involvement in the school, and practiced or supported innovative administrative or teaching techniques.[49]

And, in constructing a school quality index, the study gave 30 percent of the weight to the principal's attitude about and use of paraprofessional staff, a ranking higher than any other single factor or pair of related factors.[50]

CRITICS

In a far-ranging critique reminiscent of Bernard Barr's position (see Chapter 1), David and Laurel Tanner stated:

Bringing victims of a slum environment to the classroom in an instructional capacity can hardly be expected to provide stimulation and impetus toward learning. It can only be expected to reproduce in the classroom the previous environment of the home and the street.[51]

The racism of this statement aside, there appears to be considerable evidence contradicting the Tanners. The studies cited above included those which showed that indigenous paraprofessionals performed more effectively than professionals in ABE, tutoring, and Head Start programs. And the summary of an evaluation report by the University of Virginia School of Education on an aide training program in Buerea Vista and Lexington, Kentucky, is pertinent here.

It was shown that *the educational backgrounds of the aides were not consequential in predicting the ratings the supervising teachers would make concerning the aides.* Whether aides had completed twelve or only six years of formal schooling was not statistically significant in preassessing their competence as paraprofessional members of teaching teams. [Emphasis in the original.][52]

A Washington, D.C. program reported similar findings.

The experience of TAP [Teacher Aide Program] points to the conclusion that successful performance is not necessarily related to the aide's educational background: The group of TAP aides rated in the top 27 percent for over-all effectiveness by their teachers included some who had not completed high school.

The experience of TAP, therefore, does not weigh against drawing from the under-educated community for teacher aides. In fact, there is much to recommend this practice.[53]

A more serious charge by the Tanners is "the absence of a theoretical basis for determining the kinds of tasks they [aides] should and should not perform.[54] In a review of the literature concerning paraprofessionals, another pair of authors cited the following as a major impediment to role definition for paraprofessionals:

> [There is an] *inadequacy of current role definition for professional persons.* [It should also be noted that] *the insecurity of the supervisory professional* often places severe limitations upon the functioning of the subprofessional. [Emphasis in the original.][55]

This problem of clear role definition is pointed to in many studies, particularly the work of the Bank Street College group.[56] The Office of Education Career Opportunity Program with its emphasis on career-ladder progression will, hopefully, bring greater specificity and clarity to this area. Also, work underway at the New Careers Training Laboratory, New York University, in support of the Career Opportunity Program and in the development of a model post-secondary curriculum for teacher aides should be pertinent. Thornwald Esbensen has suggested that for aides to perform instructional tasks should not be threatening to the professional practice of teachers for

> The distinguishing characteristic of the qualified teacher is his ability to *analyze* the instructional needs of his students, and to *prescribe* the elements of formal schooling that will best meet these needs.[57]

OTHER ROLES

We have concentrated on classroom roles for paraprofessionals. But one cannot leave this topic without at least a brief mention of other roles they have played in schools. At Indian boarding schools, native "dormitory teacher aides" play a key role in bridging the gap between school and home, as well as supporting learning in a number of ways.[58] And most urban schools employ paraprofessionals in school-community liasion work.

School counseling work is an area of both particular shortage and special opportunities for indigenous workers. As Eric Ward, the director of New York City's college program for paraprofessionals, has stated,

> Experience has shown that attempts to sensitize present counselors to be more versatile in dealing with their client's problems have not resulted in as much effective communication as has the use of paraprofessionals or indigenous counselors who possess life skills that preempt their lack of formal training.[59]

Ward hard-headedly points out that the indigenous worker brings the advantage of "his ability to recognize and deal effectively with 'rationalizations'." The indigenous worker is less gullible; the professional counselor who has been "taken" by the client is less respected.[60]

Counselor programs using indigenous paraprofessionals operate in a number of communities. Detroit uses "referral assistants", Pittsburgh school attendance aides, and Baltimore pupil personnel assistants who assemble case information, participate in counseling sessions, and provide followup and referral services.

The Greenleigh Associates study described above showed that indigenous workers were the most effective in teaching ABE. A New Jersey project used paraprofessionals to design, develop, administer, and evaluate an adult education program.[61] The project used twenty-four paraprofessionals—all were poor, twelve had been on welfare, and nine had less than a high school diploma, and the others had no more education than the diploma. The workers surveyed a low-income neighborhood regarding adult-education needs, surveyed community agencies as to their programs and resources, recruited students, established an adult education program involving more than seven hundred people, and arranged for instructors and classroom facilities—one class was moved to a neighborhood bar when attendance declined at the original location—and evaluated the courses. A report on the project concluded:

> By the end of the demonstration, the trainees had designed and were conducting more than fifty different adult education courses for disadvantaged people in their own disadvantaged neighborhoods. It demonstrated that nonprofessionals can be trained to perform many of the tasks of the professional adult educator.[62]

At the Val Verde Elementary School, California, an interesting project was operated that used five different categories of nonprofessionals—housewives, college students, high school students, high school dropouts, and older elementary students. They found that each group could make special contributions to children's learning.[63]

Something of the speed with which motivated paraprofessionals can be trained to perform meaningful work is shown in an Oregon program. Low-income college students, themselves graduates of an Upward Bound program and with no prior training in education or teaching, were trained in four weeks to teach basic literacy to migrant high school dropouts in order to enable them to pass the General Education Diploma examination. Emphasis in the training was on what the trainees (college students) needed to know to teach their migrant students. At the end of the five-week High School Equivalency program (HEP), all of the students had shown significant improvement on performance measures of reading and mathematics, and 83 percent of those who took the GED test passed it.[64]

THE FUTURE

In many ways, paraprofessionals are well established in education. Increasing numbers of schools are using them, and they are demonstrating their capacity to aid pupil learning both directly and indirectly. While most programs use paraprofessionals at an entry-level position, career-development components increasingly are becoming a part of school-aide programs both as federal support increases and pressure from unionized aides mounts. (See Chapter 7.) Leon J. Keyserling predicted a rise to more than 1.1 million aides by 1972, one for every two teachers.[65] Both the National Education Association and the American Federation of Teachers have supported the use of paraprofessionals in education, and both have sought to bring them into their local structure.[66] Congressional support has been considerable, and state and local education agencies are increasingly providing funds for paraprofessional programs, making clear the statutory basis for their employment, and, as in California, enacting legislation supportive of the use of aides.[67]

An official of NEA's Teacher Education and Professional Standards Commission reported that those school systems which used paraprofessionals were also those which had at least one other innovative effort underway. He concluded "that there is some direct relationship between the use of aides and action programs to improve instruction."[68] Whether cause or no, it would appear that paraprofessionals in education may play a role even beyond the catalytic one suggested by the Bank Street College group; the role may even be synergistic.

NOTES

1. Arthur Pearl, "An Address at the Planning Conference on New Careers" (Kansas City, Missouri, 1967).

2. Alan Gartner, Mary Conway Kohler, and Frank Riessman, *Children Teach Children: Learning Through Teaching* (New York: Harper and Row, 1971).

3. *Decade of Experiment: The Fund for the Advancement of Education, 1951-61* (New York: Ford Foundation, 1961), p. 48.

4. "A Cooperative Study for the Better Utilization of Teacher Competencies" (Mount Pleasant: Central Michigan University, 1960).

5. Charles B. Park, "The Bay City Experiment . . . As Seen by the Director," *Journal of Teacher Education*, VII, 2 (June, 1956), 109.

6. *Decade of Experiment, op. cit.*, p. 50.

7. *Ibid.*, p. 51.

8. "A Symposium: The Bay City, Michigan Experiment, A Cooperative Study for the Better Utilization of Teacher Competencies," *Journal of Teacher Education*, VII, 2 (June, 1956), 110-52.

9. Barry Greenberg, "Review of Literature Relating to the Use of Nonprofessionals in Education (From 1942 to 1967)" (New York: New Careers Development Center, New York University, 1967), p. 4.

10. J. L. Trump, "A Look Ahead in Secondary Education," *National Association of Secondary School Principals Bulletin,* XLII, 234 (January, 1958), 5-15.

11. Ira J. Singer, "Survey of Staff Utilization Practices in Six States," *National Association of Secondary School Principals Bulletin,* XLVI, 270 (January, 1962), 1-11.

12. Kenneth B. Matheny and Yvonne Oslin, "Utilization of Paraprofessionals in Education and The Helping Professions: A Review of the Literature" paper presented to the American Educational Research Association, Minneapolis, March, 1970).

13. Robert Anderson, "Organizational Characteristics of Education—Staff Utilization and Development," *Review of Educational Research,* XXXIV, 4 (October, 1964), 455-66.

14. "Teacher Aides in Large School Systems" (Washington, D.C.: Research Division, National Education Association, 1967).

15. *Ibid.*; Mary D. Shipp, "Teacher Aides: A Survey," *National Elementary Principal,* XLVI, 6 (May, 1967), 30-33, "Teacher Aides in the Public Schools," *Research Bulletin,* XLV, 2 (May, 1967), 37-39, as well as XLVIII, 1 (March, 1970), 11-12; *Teacher Aides: A Status Report* (Terre Haute: School of Education, Indiana State University, 1968); California Teachers Association, *Teacher Aides in California Schools and School Districts, 1966-67,* "Research Bulletin," No. 206 (Burlingame: California Teachers Association, 1967); "Use of Teacher Aides, 1968-1969" (Washington, D.C.: Research Memo 1969-11, National Education Association, 1969); and Patti L. Lowery and William H. Denham, *New Careers: Paraprofessional Personnel in Public Education* (Washington, D.C.: National Institute for New Careers, University Research Corporation, 1970).

16. *The Education Professions, An Annual Report on the People Who Serve Our Schools and Colleges, 1969-70* (Washington, D.C.: Office of Education, U.S. Department of Health, Education, and Welfare, 1970), Tables 14, 15.

17. Arnold Glovinsky and Joseph P. Johns, "Paraprofessionals: Twenty-Six Ways to Use Them," *School Management,* XIII, 2 (February, 1966), 46-49.

18. Marilyn H. Cutler, "National Report Shows Teacher Aides Are Worth the Effort," *The Nation's Schools,* LXXIII, 4, (April, 1964), 67-69.

19. Wayne Newlin, "It Can Be Done: Teacher Aides Can Make a Difference in Illinois," *Illinois Education,* LVI, 5, (January, 1968), 213-16.

20. "How the Profession Feels About Teacher Aides," *National Education Association Journal*, LVI, 11 (November, 1967), 16-17.

21. Jack Ferver and Doris M. Cook, *Teacher Aides: A Handbook for Instructors and Administrators* (Madison: Center for Extension Programs in Education, The University of Wisconsin, 1968).

22. Alexander Mood, *Do Teachers Make a Difference? A Report on Recent Research on Pupil Achievement* (Washington, D.C.: U.S. Office of Education, 1970), p. 7.

23. *A Study of Selected Programs for the Education of Disadvantaged Children* (Palo Alto, Cal.: American Institute for Research, 1968).

24. William S. Bennett, Jr. and R. Frank Falk, *New Careers and Urban Schools* (New York: Holt, Rinehart, and Winston, 1970); Patricia Larson, "Discussions with New Careerists;" Patricia Larson, Nancye Belding, and R. Frank Falk, "A Critique of Agencies in the Minneapolis New Careers Program;" Patricia Larson *et al.*, "A Functional Model for the Use of Paraprofessional Personnel"; Patricia Larson, Mary Bible, R. Frank Falk, "Down the Up Staircase: A Study of New Careers Dropouts"; Margaret A. Thompson, "Contamination of New Careerists by Professionalization: Fact or Fancy?" and Margaret A. Thompson *et al.*, "Job Interests and Job Satisfactions of New Careerists" (Minneapolis: New Careers Research, University of Minnesota, 1969, 1968, 1968, 1969, 1969, and 1969, respectively; Margaret A. Thompson, "The Minneapolis New Careers Program: A Follow-Up Study" (Minneapolis: Office of Career Development, University of Minnesota, 1971).

25. Bennett and Falk, *op. cit.*, p. 175.

26. *Ibid.*

27. Milan B. Dady, *Director's Report: Institute for Support Personnel* (Morehead, Ky.: Morehead State University, 1970).

28. *Ibid.*

29. Nicholas J. Anastasiou, *An Evaluation of the Kindergarten Teacher Assistant Project* (Palo Alto, Cal.: Palo Alto Unified School District, 1966).

30. V. M. Ireland, *Evaluation of the Teacher Aid Program* (Atlanta: Atlanta Public Schools, 1969).

31. Timothy Wilson, "To the School Committee: Evaluative Report on Project Male" (Arlington, Mass: Memorandum to the Public Schools, June, 1970), p. 1.

32. *Ibid.*, pp. 1-2.

33. *Utilization of Paraprofessional Personnel in Intensive Remedial Reading, End of Project Report* (Hammond, Ind.: The School City of Hammond, 1970).

34. *Ibid.,* p. 47.

35. *Programmed Tutoring Follow-Up,* (Muncie: The Reading Center, School of Education, University of Indiana, 1969).

36. Lillian Pope, "Blueprint for a Successful Paraprofessional Tutorial Program," *American Journal of Orthopsychiatry,* XL, 2 (March, 1970), 299-300.

37. Donald A. Davis, "The Fennville Teacher Aide Experiment," *The Journal of Teacher Education,* XIII, 2 (June, 1962), 189.

38. *Ibid.,* p. 190.

39. Alan Gartner, *Do Paraprofessionals Improve Human Services? A First Critical Appraisal of the Data* (New York: New Careers Development Center, New York University, 1969), p. 18.

40. "Field Test and Evaluation of Selected Adult Basic Education Systems" (New York: Greenleigh Associates, Inc., 1966).

41. Elizabeth W. Brazelton, "Teacher Aide Effects on Language Development in Head Start Children" (unpublished thesis, Auburn University, 1969), p. 14.

42. James Canfield, "The High Cost of Non-Teaching Assignments," *The Clearing House,* XLIV, 5 (January, 1970), 296-99.

43. Bennett and Falk, *op. cit.,* pp. 179-80.

44. Ferver and Cook, *op. cit.,* pp. 62-63.

45. Frank C. Emerling and Kanawha Z. Chavis, "The Teacher Aide," *Educational Leadership,* XXIV, 2 (November, 1966), 177.

46. E. Erickson, *Summary Report: Teacher and Teacher Aides Studies* (Grand Rapids, Mich.: Grand Rapids Educational Studies Center, 1968).

47. Garda W. Bowman and Gordon J. Klopf, *New Careers and Roles in the American School: A Study of Auxiliary Personnel in Education* (New York: Bank Street College of Education, 1968).

48. Garda W. Bowman and Gordon J. Klopf, *Auxiliary School Personnel: Their Roles, Training, and Institutionalization* (New York: Bank Street College of Education, 1967), p. 5.

49. *Public Education in New York City* (New York: First National City Bank, 1969), p. 22.

50. *Ibid.*, Technical Appendix.

51. Daniel Tanner and Laurel N. Tanner, "Teacher Aides: A Job for Anyone in Ghetto Schools," *The Record*, LXIX, 8 (May, 1968), 788.

52. Alfred A. Arth *et al., Teacher Aides: The Preparation and Utilization of Paraprofessionals* (Charlottesville: Curry Memorial School of Education, University of Virginia, 1970), p. 41.

53. *TAP: The Teacher Aide Program* (Washington, D.C.: Washington School of Psychiatry, 1967), p. 68.

54. Tanner and Tanner, *op. cit.*, p. 744.

55. Matheny and Oslin, *op. cit.*, pp. 19-20.

56. Bowman and Klopf (1967), *op. cit.*; Bowman and Klopf (1968), *op. cit.*

57. Thornwald Esbensen, "Should Teacher Aides Be More Than Clerks?" *Phi Delta Kappan*, XLVII, 5 (January, 1966), 237.

58. Jim Wilson, "Dormitory Teacher Aides Are Big Help in South Dakota," *Journal of American Indian Education*, IX, 2 (January, 1970), 3-9.

59. Eric J. Ward, "A Gift From the Ghetto," *The Personnel and Guidance Journal*, XLVIII, 9 (May, 1970), 754.

60. *Ibid.*, p. 755.

61. Glenn M. Parker and Barry A. Passett, "The Poor Bring Adult Education to the Ghetto," *Adult Leadership*, VI, 9 (March, 1969), 327-48.

62. *Ibid.*, p. 348.

63. James R. Hartley, *Final Report: New Careers for Non-Professionals in Education* (Riverside: University of California Extension, 1965).

64. Elizabeth Rademacher, *A Training Program for Teacher Aides* (Eugene: University of Oregon, 1968).

65. Leon K. Keyserling, *Achieving Nationwide Excellence: A Ten Year Plan, 1967-77, to Save the Schools* (Washington, D.C.: Conference on Economic Progress, 1968), Table E-2.

66. Lowery and Denham, *op. cit.*, pp. 7-8; see also, *New Careers Newsletter* and *New Human Services Newsletter* (New York: New Careers Development Center, New York University), *passim.*

67. James Donald Sarwin, "Criteria for Statutory Provisions for the Employment of Teacher Aides in Public School Districts" (Denver: unpub. Ph.D. dissertation, University of Colorado, 1969); Alden Vanderpool, "California's Instructional Aide Act," *California Teachers Journal,* LXV, 2 (March, 1969), 5.

68. James L. Olivero, "Do Teacher Aides Really Aid?" *California Teachers Association Journal,* LXV, 2 (March, 1969), 35.

Unlike public schools, where paraprofessionals are relatively new (although a significant minority of the staff), in mental health programs, they are of long standing and comprise a large majority. Consideration of the paraprofessionals' role in mental health must begin with an identification: If one defines as professionals those holding postbaccalaureate professional degrees and excludes those engaged only in maintenance and housekeeping activities, one can suggest three types of paraprofessionals.

The first is the so-called old hospital-based worker. He is typified by the psychiatric aide who works in a hospital setting and is engaged in supportive, therapeutic work. He usually does not have a college degree and is not indigenous to the community in which he works; he generally comes from a low-income background and is frequently Black or Puerto Rican.

The new middle-class paraprofessional is typically a woman with a degree, who has received special training in mental health skills, and who is generally engaged in substantive, therapeutic work. Margaret Rioch's program is perhaps best known in this area. The women she trained were middle class, mainly White, and held college degrees.

Finally, there is what has been called the indigenous paraprofessional who is recruited from the community where he lives. He is usually employed, although not exclusively, in community mental health centers, does not hold a college degree, and is engaged in therapeutically relevant work.

The first type, the old paraprofessional is the most common and the heart of the staff of mental health hospital facilities. The new paraprofessional is seen in various efforts since the late 1950's to meet professional manpower shortages, while the indigenous paraprofessional is largely the child of the antipoverty and community mental health efforts. It is the last two to which we will give special attention.

THE OLD PARAPROFESSIONAL

A highly significant, well-controlled experiment conducted by Roland B. Ellsworth indicated that the old type of paraprofessional could play a powerful role in improved treatment outcome for hospitalized male schizophrenics.[1] "A demonstration project in which the focus on treatment was the development of the psychiatric aide as the rehabilitation agent" was conducted at the Veterans' Administration hospital, Fort Meade, South Dakota. Fort Meade has a 600-bed hospital; for the purposes of the demonstration, patients of one building were used as an experimental group (n = 122), and patients of two other buildings were used as a control group (n = 214). For patients in both groups, the program was similar in use of medication, use of activity-group therapy, the process of reaching decisions regarding discharge, assignment of new admissions, and patient characteristics.[2]

The demonstration program was designed to raise the level of aide-patient interaction. To do this effectively, the aide's role in the hospital had to be altered, particularly as it related to participation in decisionmaking. It was found that a higher percentage of patients from the experimental group were released to the community during the thirty-month demonstration period, and a lower percentage of them had to return to the hospital.[3]

Postdischarge outcomes were based on seven indexes: level of behavioral adjustment, median days subsequently hospitalized, released versus not released, percent achieved twelve consecutive months in the community, good social adjustment, good work adjustment, and discharge status six years later. The experimental and control groups were divided into three subgroups based on the degree of schizophrenia. There were 21 pairs of comparisons, and the experimental group did better on all 21; in thirteen of them, there was a substantial level of significance.[4] "Although the chronically hospitalized patients' group profited most by the approach used in the experimental program, the acute group of patients also responded significantly".[5]

Key factors in the aides' role seemed to be their increased interaction with patients and their more active participation in decisions regarding patients. And the two factors were interconnected "as the active involvement of the aide in the decisionmaking process was found to be a necessary condition in sustaining aide-patient interaction".[6] Ellsworth concluded:

> Our project has shown clearly that the role of a nonprofessionally trained person can be modified extensively in a psychiatric rehabilitation setting. When this modification takes the form of actively involving the nonprofessional in all phases of patient rehabilitation the treatment outcome for hospitalized male schizophrenics is highly significant.[7]

THE NEW PARAPROFESSIONAL

Perhaps best known in this area is the early work of Margaret J. Rioch and the studies of Robert R. Carkhuff and Charles B. Truax. These investigators, as well as a number of others reported in this section, provide evidence regarding the effectiveness of paraprofessionals as treatment agents.

In 1960, NIMH's Adult Psychiatry Branch funded Rioch's Mental Health Counselors program.[8] It was designed to fill the need for staff to provide low-cost psychotherapy and at the same time to provide useful work for women with grown children. The value of these women was seen in their successful child-rearing experience and maturity. There were 8 women chosen from 80 applications. Their median age was 42; 7 were married, and 1 was widowed; they had an average of 2.4 children. All were college graduates, and 3 had postbaccalaureate degrees; 6 had held professional jobs; 4 had been psychoanalyzed. All of their husbands held executive or professional positions. Their upper-class status is further shown by their ability to participate in a two-year training program without pay and with no guarantee of a job at the end of the program.

All 8 women completed the 4 semesters of training which emphasized professional breadth, not technician specificity. It was limited to psychotherapy and emphasized on-the-job training. Most of the patients of the trainees were adolescents.

Blind evaluations were made by outside experts of trainees' taped interviews with clients, and trainees were not identified as such. On a scale from 1 (poor) to 5 (excellent), the rating of the interviews on 8 factors ranged from 2.7 (beginning of interview) to 4.2 (professional attitude), with an over-all, global impression, mean score of 3.4.[9] Evaluation of patient progress (n = 49) showed that none changed for the worse, 19 percent showed no change, 61 percent showed some change. Of these, 35 percent showed slight improvement, 20 percent showed moderate improvement, and 6 percent showed marked improvement.[10] As to the counselor's faults, the director reported:

> they pleasantly reassure, protect, and sympathize when it would be better to question more deeply and seriously. A second fault is a tendency to try to deal on a surface, commonsense level with problems that are soluble only by eliciting unconscious conflicts.[11]

Similar to the Mental Health Counselors' program in terms of the background of the women trained as counselors, the Child Development Counselors' program at the Washington, D.C., Children's Hospital differed from Rioch's program in that counselors worked with patients of a different class background.[12] A similar cross-class effort was involved in the Albert Einstein College of Medicine Mental Health Rehabilitation Workers' project which also used mature women, as did a Rochester, New York, program where housewives worked with emotionally disturbed, young, school children.[13] The many programs using college students as therapeutic agents crossed both class and age lines.[14] Still other programs used peers as therapeutic agents.[15]

In Australia, paraprofessional part-time volunteers (mature adults, successfully married) provided marriage-counseling service. Some 270 persons serve approximately 15,000 persons per year. The volunteers received weekly training for about 18 months, primarily in a nondirective, client-centered,

Rogerian approach. In about 15 percent of the cases, the problem was solved; in another 25 percent of the cases, marital relations were noticeably improved, according to L. V. Harvey.[16]

Aides trained in Rogerian play therapy worked with 6 Head Start children diagnosed by a psychologist as in need of psychotherapy due to uncontrollable, withdrawn, or inhibited behavior. Each of these 6 "treated by the aide showed signs of improvement during the treatment period."[17]

Similar to these efforts is the work led by Truax at the Arkansas Rehabilitation Research and Training Center. There, the effort was made to identify those characteristics which make for more effective counseling and for the use of lay counselors. Two major experiments are of interest. The first compared the work of lay therapists, graduate-student trainees, and experienced therapists.[18] It involved 150 chronic hospitalized patients. "The variety of current diagnoses included manic depressive reactions, psychotic depressive reactions, and schizophrenic."[19] Patients were randomly assigned to lay persons who had 100 hours of training, graduate-student trainees, and experienced counselors. "The lay mental health counselors were able to provide a level of therapeutic conditions only slightly below that of the experienced therapists and considerably above that of graduate-student trainees."[20]

Earlier work of the Arkansas group had isolated three factors as critical to the therapist's effect on his patient communicating a high level of accurate empathy, nonpossessive warmth, and genuineness to the patient. There were no significant differences between the three groups of counselors as related to communicating accurate empathy or nonpossessive warmth. On the third factor, communicating genuineness to the patient, the experienced therapists showed significantly higher performance.

In his summary of the effect on patients of the work of lay therapists, Truax, as project director, wrote:

Research evaluation indicated highly significant [effects on patients] *in over-all improvement, improvement in interpersonal relations, improvement in self-care and self-concern, and improvement in emotional disturbance.* [Emphasis in the original.][21]

A second study conducted at the Arkansas Center more closely addressed the effect of paraprofessional counselors. Some 400 patients at the Hot Springs Rehabilitation Center, a large residential institution, were randomly assigned to three different groups: (a) to experienced, professional counselors with masters' degrees; (b) to experienced counselors assisted by an aide under maximum supervision; and (c) to aides (former secretaries with little if any college training) who worked alone, under supervision. Within each of the three patterns, caseload was varied at either thirty or sixty; thus, there was a 3 x 2 experimental design. Two thirds of the patients were male; two thirds were White; all had personality or behavioral problems. A sizable number had speech and hearing defects or were mentally retarded.[22]

Performance under the three patterns of staffing was measured based on the client's work quantity, cooperativeness, work attitude, work quality, dependability, ability to learn, and over-all progress. On all measures the following was noted:

The best results were obtained by the aides working alone under the daily supervision of professional counselors. The professional counselors working alone had the second-best results, while the counselor plus the aide had the poorest effects upon clients.[23]

The greater positive effects on client rehabilitation by aides with their own caseload appeared to be "due both to the somewhat higher levels of warmth and empathy communicated to the clients by the aides and the greater motivation and enthusiasm of the aides."[24]

The aides spent more time with clients, especially when they had *high* caseloads. When the professionals had high caseloads, they spent less time with clients. The aides, in effect, appeared to feel that it was necessary to work hard to get to all the cases, while the professionals seemed to feel that with so many clients to see, what was the use. However: "Over-all, neither the total number of minutes spent in contact with individual clients nor the frequency of client contacts was related to the client vocational progress."[25] In carrying their conclusions beyond this project, the authors stated:

The findings presented here are consistent with a growing body of research which indicates that the effectiveness of counseling and psychotherapy, as measured by constructive changes in client functioning, is largely independent of the counselor's level of training and theoretical orientation.[26]

The broadest examination of the work of paraprofessionals in mental health is Francine Sobey's study of over 10,000 paraprofessionals in 185 NIMH-sponsored programs.[27] As data were presented in gross categories, one cannot, for the most part, distinguish the particular type of paraprofessional being employed, although it would seem that they included persons from all three of the groups delineated above—the old, the new middle-class, and the indigenous paraprofessional. Sobey's major findings related to the reason for the use of paraprofessionals.

Nonprofessionals are utilized not simply because professional manpower is unavailable but rather to provide new services in innovative ways. Nonprofessionals are providing such therapeutic functions as individual counseling, activity group therapy, milieu therapy; they are doing case finding; they are playing screening roles of a nonclerical nature; they are helping people to adjust to community life; they are providing special skills such as tutoring; they are promoting client self-help through involving clients in helping others having similar problems.[28]

The basis for the use of paraprofessionals is illustrated in Table 6 by the response of project directors to the question as to whether, given a choice of hiring professionals, they would prefer to utilize paraprofessionals for those functions which professionals had previously performed.[29] In short, 53 percent of the directors preferred to use paraprofessionals over professionals for tasks previously performed by professionals, or, to state it another way, only 32

TABLE 6

Utilization Preference for Professionals or Nonprofessionals

Utilization Preference	Number of Project Directors Responding
Would clearly utilize professional staff	17
Would probably utilize professional staff	38
Uncertain	29
Would probably not utilize professional staff	36
Would clearly not utilize professional staff	55

Note: Responses were from directors of projects funded by the National Institute of Mental Health.

Source: Francine Sobey, *The Nonprofessional Revolution in Mental Health* (New York: Columbia University Press, 1970), pp. 155-6.

percent preferred to use professionals. As could be anticipated from the above, "Overwhelmingly the project directors felt that the service performed by nonprofessionals justified the expense of training, supervision, and general agency overhead."[30]

The directors saw paraprofessionals contributing across a broad spectrum of program activities which included servicing more people, offering new services, and providing the project staff with new viewpoints in regard to the project population.[31] Table 7 displays the directors' evaluations of these contributions. The response to the last item in Table 7 relating to new viewpoints suggests that a significant number of paraprofessionals were indigenous workers. Also, in 69 projects, the directors reported expanding professional staff understanding of the client group through association with paraprofessionals.[32] The same thrust is to be seen in the comment: "The introduction of nonprofessionals was perceived as infusing the projects with a new vitality, and forcing a self-evaluation which, although painful, led to beneficial changes for the field of mental health."[33] The work style and personal attributes of paraprofessionals were also important.

[They brought] a change in atmosphere within the agency, and more lively and vital relationships among staff and between patients and staff. . . . Improved morale, better attitudes toward patients, definite improvement in over-all quality of service were other improvements reported. The addition of youthful, untrained personnel within several hospitals makes the older trained personnel reexamine their own roles and the role, structure, and function of the entire hospital.[34]

In summary, Sobey noted:

TABLE 7

Contributions by Nonprofessionals to Improvements in Service

| Improvements in Service | Projects Reporting Degree of Nonprofessional Contribution (in percent) | | | Total Number of Project Responses |
	Substantial	Moderate	Slight or Not at All	
Service initiated/completed faster	54	31	15	80
Able to serve more people	59	32	8	127
New services provided	57	27	16	141
More professional time made available for treatment	45	31	24	106
New viewpoints gained by project staff repopulation served	53	31	16	135

Source: Francine Sobey, *The Nonprofessional Revolution in Mental Health* (New York: Columbia University Press, 1970), p. 160.

47

Nonprofessionals were viewed as contributing to mental health in two unique ways: (1) *filling new roles based on patient needs* which were previously unfilled by any staff; and (2) performing parts of tasks previously performed by professionals, but *tailoring the task to the nonprofessionals' unique and special abilities.* [Emphasis added.][35]

The value of the use of new paraprofessionals is summarized by Carkhuff, a former staff member of the Arkansas Center.

In directly comparable studies, selected lay persons with or without training and/or supervision have patients who demonstrate changes as great or greater than the patients of professional practitioners.[36]

THE INDIGENOUS PARAPROFESSIONAL

The characteristics of the lay counselor, as described by Carkhuff, appear to apply as well to the indigenous worker. These include the following six characteristics: (a) the increased ability to enter the milieu of the distressed; (b) the ability to establish peerlike relationships with the needy; (c) the ability to take an active part in the clients' total life situation; (d) the ability to empathize more fully with the clients' style of life; (e) the ability to teach the client, from within the clients' frame of reference, more successful actions; and (f) the ability to provide clients with a more effective transition to more effective levels of functioning within the social system.[37]

One of the earliest uses of indigenous paraprofessionals was at Howard University in the Baker's Dozen project of Jacob R. Fishman, Lonnie E. Mitchell, and colleagues.[38] The Howard team's work has continued both there and at the University Research Corporation, where many reports include consideration of mental health programs, primarily as part of New Careers efforts.

A 1969 survey of 80 community mental health centers found that 42 percent of all full-time positions were filled by indigenous workers. The figures were higher in drug-abuse treatment (60%) and geriatric services (70%).[39] In the same year, a study of paraprofessionals in 10 community mental health centers in New York City reported their "actual work as described by administrators varied from unskilled to highly skilled but more often is of the highly skilled variety."[40] The work included interviewing, escort service, home visits, manning storefront offices, receiving complaints, collecting information, acting as translators, performing individual and group counseling, organizing community meetings, leading therapy groups, assisting patients in self-care, acting as patients' advocates with other agencies, casefinding, screening applicants, making case conference presentations, doing casework, giving speeches, planning aftercare services, and giving supportive psychotherapy to former patients.[41]

Robert Reiff and Frank Riessman made the point that the use of indigenous paraprofessionals is part of the new concern for service to the poor.

If the concern is only to meet professional manpower shortages, indigenousness is unnecessary. However, if there is a concern to reach and serve those unreached and unserved, in short, if the propelling motive grows out of a critique of service performance, then the indigenous worker may be needed.[42] The ability of indigenous paraprofessionals is "rooted in their background. It is not based on things they have been taught, but on what they *are*."[43] They are poor, from the neighborhood, minority-group members, from poor families, and they share common language, background, ethnic origin, style, and interests with the client.* They can establish special relations with clients—the paraprofessional belongs, he is a significant other, he is one of us. His life-style is similar to that of the client, especially "the tendency to externalize causes rather than look for internal ones."[44]

Emanuel Hallowitz, codirector of the pioneering Lincoln Hospital Mental Health Services Neighboorhood Service Center program, described a range of activities for the indigenous worker in such a setting. These included expediting, being a friend in need, sociotherapy, supervised work, services to post-hospital patients, services to the disturbed in the community, and self-help.[45]

The Lincoln Hospital Mental Health Services Neighborhood Service Center program began with an OEO grant, January 1, 1965. Three centers, each staffed with five to ten aides, were established; they were seen as bridges between the professionals and the community. There were expediters, advocates, and counselors. Something of the power of their impact and the need for services in a community such as the South Bronx is shown by the service figure of 6,500 persons seen at two of the centers in the first nine months. The program offered services to the clients' whole family, and it was estimated that over 25,000 persons were actually saved during that period.[46]

Harlem Hospital also employed indigenous workers in a variety of roles. Harlem residents, interested in working with the aged, provided outpatient geriatric psychiatric services. They made home visits, provided escort services, observed and reported on patient behavior, and provided social services. About half of the study group of sixty cases were successfully managed.

Especially innovative was June Jackson Christmas' Harlem Hospital Group Therapy Program, which used indigenous aides.[47] The aides worked in a half-day treatment program for a small group of chronic, psychotic, posthospital patients. The aides participated as cotherapists in weekly group psychotherapy sessions, acted as participants and expediters in the monthly medication group meetings, were members of the weekly therapeutic community meetings, and led the weekly client discussion groups. In addition, they performed case services, family services, home interviews, surveyed patient needs, and provided community mental health education.[48] The program was expected to hold one third of the patients; it has held two thirds.[49] A four-step

---

*Perhaps the ultimate in the use of the indigenous worker is an NIMH-funded project to train twelve Navajo males as medicine men. They are to learn the fifty ceremonies of tribal traditions for treating illness and to work with the Public Health Service doctors re referrals and assistance.

career ladder—trainee, worker, technician, specialist—is in effect, gained, in part, through the efforts of Local 1199 of the Drug and Hospital Workers Union.[50]

The Temple University Community Mental Health Center also trained indigenous workers as mental health assistants, workers who they described as "helpers first, then therapists."[51] Over time, a work pattern developed where the mental health assistants "function as a 'primary therapist' providing ongoing treatment and continuity of care which would include the procurement of ancillary [professional] services whenever appropriate."[52] The assistants, a title the workers themselves preferred to aide, worked with 96 percent of the patients in the clinic's first year. Two key factors in their work involved "holding" patients, and, by their availability, preventing hospitalization.

> While the percentage of patients' attrition between initial contact and first appointment is still high, it is a lower rate than that presented for comparable patient aggregates in usual clinic settings. The need to hospitalize patients contacting the crisis center and clinic has decreased by 50 percent due to the assistants' availability for immediate outpatient care.[53]

The Central City Community Mental Health Center, in Los Angeles, used community workers in a program designed to develop additional mental health manpower, train new workers, improve understanding between the disadvantaged and mental health personnel, increase available services, and create new services appropriate to the disadvantaged. Community workers were used in the mental health facility itself, at a family service center, in various social welfare agencies, in a public health project, in a public housing program, and in providing crisis intervention therapy in a suicide prevention program.[54]

Indigenous paraprofessionals in mental health programs serve in a variety of ways. Some of these are as alcoholism counselors in a program of the Baltimore County Health Department; as paramedic technicians at a state residential school for the mentally retarded in Hawaii; as part of a home-treatment team at the Veterans' Administration Hospital in Tuscaloosa, Alabama; and in a child guidance clinic component of a comprehensive mental health center in Rochester, New York.[55]

FORMAL EDUCATION AND PERFORMANCE

In a far-reaching study of 17 state rehabilitation agencies which involved 209 counselors, 50 supervisors and 1,502 patients, the ratings of supervisors and patients were correlated with four levels of worker education—post-master's degree, master's degree, bachelor's degree, and less than a bachelor's degree.[56]

> [H]igher levels of academic training of rehabilitation counselors do not result in higher supervisor ratings on the dimension of over-all effectiveness of the counselor.

[H]igher levels of academic training for rehabilitation counselors do not result in higher client reports of satisfaction with his counselor.[57]

The lack of correlation between formal education and work performance has been cited in many of the reports described above. It may be that the type of formal education presently offered does not lead to improved paraprofessional performance because, as we have seen, training of untrained people has led to improved performance. New training approaches are beginning to develop at the college level.

Something of a new approach is being developed in the new mental health college programs. In 1965, a NIMH grant inaugurated (at Purdue University) the first two-year training program for mental health workers.[58] This was followed, in 1966, by a Southern Regional Education Board conference on the role of community colleges in mental health training. In 1967, two Maryland community colleges began such programs.[59] By September, 1968, twenty-six community colleges were offering similar programs, and there were fifty-seven by 1970. The programs emphasize practicum, interviewing skills, counseling, use of community resources, and techniques of behavior modification.[60] In evaluating the Purdue program, various effects have been noted as regards changes in patient care—humanizing the hospital, opening closed wards, establishing patient government, increased use of recreation and work facilities, and use of new treatment modalities such as milieu therapy and sociotherapy.[61]

These developments offer some countervailing tendencies to the findings of the survey of New York City community mental health centers (described above), that despite the fact that 70 percent of the center administrators rated the paraprofessional contribution as essential and another 22 percent rated it highly desirable, there is "little thought given toward developing the paraprofessional job into a worthwhile one".[62]

And, perhaps, encouraging is the fact that the graduates of the new Purdue program, while working in mental health facilities, have not chosen to do so in traditional mental health facilities. It may be, as the authors suggest, that these workers are disillusioned with the traditional medical model of mental health services.[63]

The tensions involved between new personnel, new training, and traditional mental health practices were well captured in a far-reaching article by Salvador Minuchin. He pointed out that initially the use of paraprofessionals in mental health grew out of the manpower shortage.

For many professionals, a very important major assumption was implicit in this strategy; that we could maintain intact the traditional conceptualizations of mental illness and treatment, simply fitting the nonprofessional into the already existing structure of delivery of service. But the inclusion of paraprofessionals in the existing structure of delivery of service brought to a head a bipolarity of approaches to mental illness which was already incipient in the field.[64]

At the one pole, where sociological thinking has dominated, where pathology is seen as coming from the outside in, paraprofessionals have had less difficulty in fitting in. At the other pole, when the individual is very much a separate human being, the problem of fitting in has been far greater. Hence, there are those who see paraprofessionals as doing little more than "implementing the professional's recommendations and their supervision."[65]

Minuchin's answer is that the field itself must be changed and indeed, the very relationship of individual and society, reconceptualized.[66] As we have seen, the paraprofessional, initially introduced in a narrow framework, has, in one way or another, become a force for and focus around changes of a basic nature in the field. It is these changes, rather than minor tinkering within the present structure, which may be the shapers of the paraprofessionals' future role in mental health.

SUMMARY

The wide range of data on traditional, old paraprofessionals working in hospitals, new middle-class paraprofessionals, and indigenous paraprofessionals all indicate in various ways that paraprofessionals can play a role in the rehabilitation and treatment of patients. Probably not one of these studies is conclusive in itself, although a number of them such as those by Ellsworth, Truax, Sobey, and at Temple do individually offer rather powerful evidence. However, the point is that the multiplicity of evidence derived from a great variety of sources, stemming from different investigator biases, and using diverse methods and indexes, leads to the conclusion that paraprofessionals play an important role as treatment agents and contribute to the improved mental health of clients and patients in highly significant, often unique ways.

NOTES

1. Roland B. Ellsworth, *Nonprofessionals in Psychiatric Rehabilitation* (New York: Appleton-Century-Crofts, 1968).

2. *Ibid.*, p. 87.

3. *Ibid.*, p. 162.

4. *Ibid.*, p. 161.

5. *Ibid.*, p. 164.

6. *Ibid.*, p. 165.

7. *Ibid.*

8. Margaret J. Rioch *et al.*, "National Institute of Mental Health Pilot Study in Training Mental Health Counselors," *American Journal of Orthopsychiatry*, XXXIII, 4 (July, 1963), 678-89.

9. *Ibid.*, pp. 683-84.

10. *Ibid.*, p. 685.

11. *Ibid.*, p. 688.

12. Carl Eisdorfer and Stuart E. Golann, "Principles for the Training of 'New Professionals' in Mental Health," *Community Mental Health Journal*, V, 5 (May, 1969), 357.

13. Ida F. Davidoff *et al.*, "The Mental Health Rehabilitation Worker: A New Member of the Psychiatric Team," *Community Mental Health Journal*, V, 1 (January, 1969), 46-54.

14. Emory L. Cowen *et al.*, "A College Student Volunteer Program in the Elementary School Setting," *Community Mental Health Journal*, II, 4 (Winter, 1966), 319-28; Jules Holzberg *et al.*, "Chronic Patients and a College Companion Program," *Mental Hospitals*, XV, 3 (March, 1964), 152-58; S. F. Kreitzer, "The Therapeutic Use of Student Volunteers," in Bernard F. Guerney, Jr., ed., *Psychotherapeutic Agents: New Roles for Nonprofessionals, Parents, and Teachers* (New York: Holt, Rinehart, and Winston, 1969); William E. Mitchell, "Amica Therapy: Theoretical Perspectives and an Example of Practice," *Community Mental Health Journal*, II, 4 (Winter, 1966), 307-14; Helen Reinherz, "The Therapeutic Use of Student Volunteers," *Children*, II, 4 (April, 1964); 137-42.

15. Bernard F. Guerney, Jr., ed., *Psychotherapeutic Agents: New Roles for Nonprofessionals, Parents, and Teachers* (New York: Holt, Rinehart, and Winston, 1969), Part 4.

16. L. V. Harvey, "The Use of Nonprofessional Auxiliary Counselors in Staffing a Counseling Service," *Journal of Counseling Psychology*, XI, 4 (Winter, 1964), 348-51.

17. Michael P. Androvic and Bernard Guerney, Jr., "A Psychotherapeutic Aide in a Head Start Program, Part I, Theory and Practice," *Children*, XVI, 1 (January-February, 1969), 16.

18. Charles B. Truax, "An Approach Toward Training for the Aide-Therapist: Research and Implications" (Fayetteville: Arkansas Rehabilitation Research and Training Center, 1965).

19. *Ibid.*, p. 10.

20. *Ibid.*, p. 9.

21. *Ibid.*, p. 12.

22. Charles B. Truax and James L. Lister, "Effectiveness of Counselors and Counselor Aides," *Journal of Counseling Psychology*, XVII, 4 (July, 1970), 331-32.

23. *Ibid.*, p. 333.

24. Charles B. Truax, "The Use of Supportive Personnel in Rehabilitation Counseling" (Fayetteville: Arkansas Rehabilitation Research and Training Center, n.d.), p. 28.

25. *Ibid.*

26. Truax and Lister, *op. cit.*, p. 334.

27. Francine Sobey, *The Nonprofessional Revolution in Mental Health* (New York: Columbia University Press, 1970).

28. *Ibid.*, p 6.

29. *Ibid.*, pp. 155-56.

30. *Ibid.*, p. 154.

31. *Ibid.*, p. 159.

32. *Ibid.*, p. 161.

33. *Ibid.*, p. 175.

34. *Ibid.*, p. 160.

35. *Ibid.*, p. 174.

36. Robert R. Carkhuff, "Differential Functioning of Lay and Professional Helpers," *Journal of Counseling Psychology*, XV, 2 (March, 1968) 119.

37. *Ibid.*, pp. 121-22.

38. Jacob R. Fishman and John McCormack, "Mental Health Without Walls: Community Mental Health in the Ghetto," *American Journal of Psychiatry*, CXXVI, 10 (April, 1970), 1461-67; Jacob R. Fishman and Lonnie E. Mitchell, "New Careers for the Disadvantaged" (paper presented at the Annual Meeting of the American Psychiatric Association, (San Francisco: May 18, 1970); Lonnie E. Mitchell *et al.*, "Baker's Dozen: A Program for Training Young People as Mental Health Aides," *Mental Health Program Reports*, II

(National Institute for Mental Health, 1968), 11-24; Lonnie E. Mitchell *et al.*, *Training for Community Mental Health Aides: Leaders for Child and Adolescent Therapeutic Activity Groups: Reports of a Program* (Washington, D.C.: Institute for Youth Studies, Howard University, 1966).

39. National Institute for New Careers, *New Careers in Mental Health: A Status Report* (Washington, D.C.: University Research Corporation, 1970), pp. 14-15.

40. Harry Gottesfeld *et al.*, "A Study of the Role of Paraprofessionals in Community Mental Health," *Community Mental Health Journal*, VI, 4 (April, 1970), 286.

41. *Ibid.*

42. Robert Reiff and Frank Riessman, *The Indigenous Nonprofessional: A Strategy of Change in Community Action and Community Mental Health Programs* (New York: National Institute of Labor Education, 1964), p. 6.

43. *Ibid.*, p. 8.

44. *Ibid.*, pp. 9-10.

45. Emanuel Hallowitz, "The Expanding Role of the Neighborhood Service Center," in Frank Riessman and Hermine I. Popper, eds., *Up From Poverty: New Career Ladders for Nonprofessionals* (New York: Harper and Row, 1968), pp. 94-101.

46. Frank Riessman and Emanuel Hallowitz, "Neighborhood Service Center Program," a report to the U.S. Office of Economic Opportunity on the South Bronx Neighborhood Service Center, December, 1965, pp. 1-7.

47. June Jackson Christmas, "Group Methods in Teaching and Practice: Nonprofessional Mental Health Personnel in a Deprived Community," *American Journal of Orthopsychiatry*, XXXVI, 3 (April, 1966), 410-19.

48. *Ibid.*, pp. 413-14.

49. Ruth Wade *et al.*, "The View of the Paraprofessional," *American Journal of Orthopsychiatry*, XXXIX, 4 (July, 1969), 678.

50. National Institute for New Careers, *op. cit.*, p. 13.

51. Mary Lynch *et al.*, "The Role of Indigenous Personnel as Clinical Therapists," *Archives of General Psychiatry*, XIX, 4 (October, 1968), 428-34.

52. *Ibid.*, p. 429.

53. *Ibid.*, p. 430.

54. National Institute for New Careers, *op. cit.*, p. 12.

55. *Ibid.*, pp. 12, 14; *New York Times*, January 11, 1970, p. 63; *New York Times*, January 16, 1970, p. 34.

56. James R. Engelkes and Ralph R. Roberts, "Rehabilitation Counselor's Level of Training and Job Performance," *Journal of Counseling Psychology*, XVII, 6 (November, 1970), 522-66.

57. *Ibid.*, p. 524.

58. Alfred M. Wellner and Ralph Simon, "A Survey of Associate Degree Programs for Mental Health Technicians," *Hospital and Community Psychiatry*, XX, 6 (June, 1969), 168.

59. Robert M. Vidaver, "The Mental Health Technician: Maryland's Design for a New Health Career," *American Journal of Orthopsychiatry*, CXXV, 8 (February, 1969), 1014.

60. Wellner and Simon, *op. cit.*, pp. 28-29.

61. John Hadley *et al.*, "An Experiment in the Education of the Preprofessional Mental Health Worker: The Purdue Program," *Community Mental Health Journal*, VI, 1 (February, 1970), 42.

62. Gottesfeld *et al., op. cit.*, p. 289.

63. Wellner and Simon, *op. cit.*, p. 30.

64. Salvador Minuchin, "The Paraprofessional and the Use of Confrontation in the Mental Health Field," *American Journal of Orthopsychiatry*, XXXIX, 5 (October, 1969), pp. 722-29.

65. *Ibid.*, p. 724.

66. *Ibid.*, p. 728.

4

The paraprofessional in social work differs from those in the field of education, where most personnel are professionals. In social work, most of those in the field do not possess professional degrees. Only some one in four social-welfare workers have had two or more years of professional training, and the figures balloon to one in twenty in the largest field employing social workers, public assistance. And even if graduate school enrollments were to double (a most unlikely development), this would barely meet replacement needs.[1] Thus, the position, status, and role of professionals is affected in a field where many nonprofessionals—that is, those not holding master's degrees in the field—have done and continue to do the professionals' job.[2]

NEW MANPOWER

The need for additional manpower was felt earlier in social work than in other fields, and both experiments using and efforts at a conceptual framework for integrating paraprofessionals were undertaken. The St. Louis Hospital developed a social health technician program, in 1955; the Arden House Seminar on Case Work With the Aging, in 1960, gave much attention to the topic, as did the NASW Subcommittee on Utilization of Personnel, in 1962; and in the same year, the Veterans' Administration (VA) conducted a pilot study on the use of social-work technicians.[3] In 1962, two articles appeared in the major journal of the field, *Social Work*, published by the key professional organization, NASW, devoted to developing a theoretical schema for understanding the role of paraprofessionals and fitting them into existing organizational patterns.[4] This effort at conceptualization of the role of these workers was the first in any field.

In 1961, an experiment was conducted in a Cleveland private agency for the aged. Three college graduates worked with professional caseworkers as team members, and the team carried a higher caseload as a result.[5] The assistant provided continuing, direct services to the client to augment and supplement those of the professional, as well as activities of direct assistance to casework, e.g., information gathering and appointment making. The project was evaluated in three areas.

> Effect upon the client—The teamwork of the professional and nonprofessional personnel does result in more complete service for client than is true when the professional person working alone must make choices within available time as to emphasis and services within a given case load. . . .
>
> Clarity of role division—It is quite possible to differentiate and coordinate the two roles of caseworkers and assistant without confusing the client. . . .
>
> Number served—Caseloads were increased from the 40 served by the professional alone to 75 with the assistant.[6]

Paraprofessionals (here, those with less than college degrees) were used as aides in the Chicago Travelers Aid Society.[7] The program offered protective travel services, crisis assistance, and social-treatment planning. Professionals were usually assigned cases of the last group, paraprofessionals the first, and crisis intervention was shared. The over-all result of major professional significance was the unit's greatly increased capacity for concentrating its trained staff on producing not only an increased quantity but a higher quality of specific casework services in reaching a most difficult and disturbed group of clients.[8]

A study of paraprofessionals used in twelve foster family care agencies in New York City noted that paraprofessionals offered such supportive services as friendly visiting, including serving as escorts and caring for children; administrative, through information disemination; and enriching, through tutoring or recreation.[9] After the director noted that the paraprofessionals performed well, he said:

> In fact, in 25 percent of the case situations, supervisors said their expectation for service would have been the same as if a professional worker had been working with the client or foster mother.[10]

Quite similar findings were reported by the Pre-Professional Training Project conducted among eighteen child-planning agencies in New York City.

> Most agencies participating in the project found that these workers carried caseloads approximately two thirds of the regular loads carried by the professional worker and that this justified the outlay of effort and expense. . . . Agencies were unanimous in concluding that the workers played a substantial role in providing coverage.[11]

The conclusion of the above-cited studies, as well as many others, is that much of what professional social workers do is being done and *can be done* by paraprofessionals.[12] Most dramatic is the report in an NASW-sponsored monograph that social work assistants were able to perform 80-90 percent of the direct service tasks previously performed by professionals.[13] In addition, and of equal interest to this study, the work performed by these paraprofessionals did not call upon any special characteristics or qualities which they possessed.

THE INDIGENOUS PARAPROFESSIONAL

In a summary of experience from the late 1950's and early 1960's, George Brager, codirector of MFY, the agency which took a leading role in the shift to indigenous paraprofessionals, wrote:

> There is widespread agreement that auxiliary personnel ought to be used as assistants to relieve the heavy work load of the harassed social worker. There is also considerable, although less widespread, sentiment for the development of a "social work assistant" position, requiring independent functioning. Both "solutions" presuppose well-educated technicians who, although less well trained and experienced than the professional, function essentially in his image. By definition they must be middle-class.[14]

There had been a few efforts to use nonmiddle-class paraprofessionals in periods before the 1960's. In a report on the Chicago Area Project, an antideliquency program, 1935-59, the use of indigenous workers was described and was justified by their knowledge of the local society, the absence of barriers to communication with residents, the fact that their employment demonstrated confidence in the area residents' capabilities, their access to the neighborhood's delinquent youth, and its effect as a way to educate members of the local population.[15] Other antidelinquency programs in the early 1960's used paraprofessionals as street workers, counselors, and so forth. (See Chapter 1 and Chapter 6.) As concern with poverty grew, the value of employment opportunities for low-income persons was seen. And, as interest in meeting the service needs of the poor increased, the value to the helper of giving help was highlighted.[16]

Brager, however, based his call for the use of the indigenous paraprofessional on the value to be gained "from the possibility that low-income persons might perform program tasks."[17] He noted that except for reference to the Chicago Area Project, and unpublished papers by Gertrude Goldberg and Frank Riessman, there had been no discussion in the professional literature of such a use of indigenous workers. In fact, by the time Brager's article was published, at least two pieces had appeared that made major reference to the program contributions which could be made by indigenous workers.[18] More important than exact dating, however, was the appearance of Brager's pioneering article. Brager cited a number of program goals achievable through the employment of the indigenous paraprofessional.

[I] ncreases the meaningful participation of *other* slum dwellers in social welfare and community programs. This due to the greater ease of contact, communication, and support on the part of the indigenous workers.

[T] he social climate of the service may be affected significantly by drawing persons *from* and *of* the community, representative of the style, various needs, and wants of the community's low income residents.

Builds two-way "bridges" between agency and community to be served as they perform a "social-class mediating" function.

Provide viable role models.[19]

For goals such as these to be achieved, the role of the indigenous worker must have a degree of validity in its own right and not merely be the residue of "shredding out" the less "professional" or desirable parts of the work of a master's degree holder.

An example of the effect of the indigenous worker was seen in a voter-registration drive conducted by MFY. "Both professionals and nonprofessionals did extensive door-to-door canvassing, with dramatic differences in achievement; the extensive success of the nonprofessionals was matched by the extensive failure of the professionals."[20]

The most extensive nationwide use of indigenous workers in a social welfare program was Project Enable, a joint venture of the Urban League, the Family Service Association, and the Child Study Association, which was funded by OEO.[21] Indigenous workers in fifty-nine communities recruited poverty-neighborhood parents for parent-education groups, identified local problems, conducted research interviews, disseminated information about the project, and acted as expediters for participants' problems. Two of the project's senior staff concluded: "Nonprofessional neighborhood workers can be rapidly trained on the job to perform a variety of meaningful, satisfying, and essential tasks effectively." And the project's final report stated: "Project Enable demonstrated that low-income people, without prior training or experience, could simultaneously serve the community and receive on-the-job training. The social welfare client can become the helper."[22]

The paraprofessional project that was most carefully reported on was conducted as a two-year demonstration by the Alameda County Welfare Department.[23] There were 14 paraprofessionals between the ages of 27 and 46; all had been on welfare, ranging from 2 to 16 years, with an average of 7 years; they had had between 6 and 12 years of schooling; 13 were Black; and all but one completed the ten-week training program. They were "chosen specifically for their lack of vocational skills, poor work history, and limited education."[24]

Their work assignments were designed to draw on the paraprofessionals' past experience of living in a poverty area and raising a family on a limited income. During the course of the project, they worked with approximately 450 caseworkers and served some 2,900 clients. They worked in the Family Services, Intake, Employment Rehabilitation Services, Child Welfare, and Adult Services programs. Table 8 describes how their time was spent, by type of service requested of them.[25] The activities tabulated in Table 8 alone cannot give a full picture of the paraprofessionals' work. Regardless of the nature of the request, the paraprofessional was likely to offer advice, give tips, and provide information to clients. "They take time to first talk to clients."[26]

TABLE 8

Activities of Welfare-Case Aides, by Time and Service Requested

Percent of Time	Type of Service Activity Requested
20	Specialized counseling in homemaking, child care, money management, use of community resources, and so forth
40	Concrete services such as finding housing, providing emergency transportation, getting free goods
32	Establishing and maintaining eligibility
6	Renewal or review visits
2	Giving information regarding welfare policies and services

Source: Dorthea Cudaback, "Summary Report in Welfare Service Aide Project" (Richmond: School of Social Work, University of California, 1968, mimeographed), p. 4.

The caseworkers' reasons for making referrals to the paraprofessionals cover a broad range of factors: (a) Paraprofessionals' special knowledge, (b) lack of time of workers to provide service, (c) another viewpoint desired, (d) lack of racial or class barrier between the paraprofessional and the client, and (e) paraprofessionals' "gut level" approach to services.[27] In summary, the project's director concluded:

> [Welfare] clients who have lived and raised families in poverty areas can as welfare department employees provide significantly valuable services to other clients. [As] coworkers with the White middle-class graduates who comprise the bulk of our line welfare workers, they can bridge the communications barriers between the welfare department "establishment" and the ghetto.[28]

The indigenous paraprofessional may then have an effect not only on the agency's clients but on its workers. A report on the effect of Project Enable noted the impact on both staff and board members.

> The aides, perhaps more than any others, helped staff and board members see the poor as people. [And for the workers in particular,]

without exception, they state that the experience contributed to their personal and professional growth. Their feelings and attitudes were altered. Group and community organization skills were developed or greatly enhanced.[29]

Communication is a key issue, for here, perhaps as nowhere else, the indigenous worker is a challenge to the professional social worker. Harry Specht stated:

The new careerist, born and raised in the lower-income life and style so different from the middle-class professional's, implicitly, if not explicitly, challenges the organization's morally buttressed *modus operandi.*[30]

In another study, Fred M. Loewenberg noted:

[N] onprofessionals often question social worker's basic assumptions, some resent the professional's method, and others challenge the commitment of the professionally trained staff.[31]

And Brager stated:

[Indigenous nonprofessionals] see barriers to the resolution of individual and community-wide problems stemming from organizational rigidity or disinterest. [They are] less interested in or sensitive to the maintenance requirements of the agency that employs them.[32]

Some have questioned the degree of indigeneity of these workers as, for example, Charles G. Grosser, who reported that MFY indigenous workers ranked closer on an attitude scale to the MFY professionals than to the client population.[33] Others have expressed doubt as to the value of indigeneity, as Sherman Barr's comments indicated.[34] That there are clear differences between the indigenous worker and the professional is amply attested by experience in the field. In an attempt to cut through the miasma of efforts to distinguish between professional and nonprofessional, Specht and his colleagues (themselves indigenous paraprofessionals, which may account for their uncommon directness in a professional journal article), said that the differences were not to be seen in terms of the tasks performed, as they were essentially the same for both professionals and paraprofessionals: "Ultimately [the distinction will have to rest] on the extent of knowledge different workers bring to their tasks and the degree of skill with which they perform them."[35] In part, perhaps, it may be that "different workers" bring different sets of knowledge and skills to their tasks. A report on the work of the Unified Social Service Project of New Haven's antipoverty program stated:

[The] combination of professional and paraprofessional in a social-service team would provide the most effective kind of service.

[This is supported by two major findings.]

Given the same number of contacts with clients, teams consisting of a professional social worker and either a paraprofessional homemaker adviser or neighborhood worker were more successful in solving clients' problems than a team of professionals or paraprofessionals alone.

Such teams achieved positive results with fewer contacts than social workers operating independently.[36]

While there is much to question in the professional practice of social work, there may well be the possibility of a symbiotic process at work between the experiences, insights, and skills of the indigenous paraprofessional and the knowledge and training of the social worker.

NOTES

1. Henrik L. Blum *et al.*, "The Multi-Purpose Worker and the Neighborhood Multi-Service Center: Initial Experience and Implications of the RODEO Community Service Center," *American Journal of Public Health*, LVIII, 3 (March, 1968), 458.

2. Robert L. Barker and Thomas L. Briggs, *Differential Use of Social Work Manpower* (New York: National Association of Social Workers, 1968), p. 53.

3. Marcella Farrar and Mary L. Hemmy, "Use of Nonprofessional Staff in Work with the Aged," *Social Work*, VIII, 3 (July, 1963), 44.

4. W. L. Richan, "A Theoretical Scheme for Determining Roles of Professional and Nonprofessional Personnel," *Social Work*, VI, 4 (October, 1961), 22-28; Verne Weed and William H. Denham, "Toward More Effective Use of the Nonprofessional Worker: A Recent Experiment," *Social Work*, VI, 4 (October, 1961), 29-36.

5. Farrar and Hemmy, *op. cit.*, pp. 44-48.

6. *Ibid.*, p. 47.

7. Laura Epstein, "Differential Use of Staff: A Method to Expand Social Services," *Social Work*, VII, 4 (October, 1962), 66-72.

8. *Ibid.*, p. 72.

9. Betty Lacy Jones, "Nonprofessional Workers in Professional Foster Family Agencies," *Child Welfare*, XLV, 6 (June, 1966), 313-25.

10. *Ibid.*, p. 320.

11. Weed and Denham, *op. cit.*, p. 33.

12. Samuel Mencher, "Social Policy and Welfare Manpower," in Edward E. Schwartz, ed., *Manpower in Social Welfare: Research Perspectives* (New York: National Association of Social Workers, 1966), *passim*.

13. Barker and Briggs, *loc. cit.*

14. George Brager, "The Indigenous Worker: A New Approach for the Social Work Technician," *Social Work*, X, 2 (April, 1965), 33-40.

15. Solomon Kobrin, "The Chicago Area Project: A Twenty-Five Year Assessment," *Annals of the American Academy of Political and Social Science*, CCCXLI (March, 1959), 19-29.

16. Reissman's article on the "helper-therapy" principle was in the same issue of *Social Work* as the Brager article, *op. cit.*, which was the first mention in that key journal of the indigenous nonprofessional; see Frank Riessman, "The 'Helper-Therapy' Principle," *Social Work*, X, 2 (April, 1965), 27-32.

17. Brager, *op. cit.*, p. 34.

18. Robert Reiff and Frank Riessman, *The Indigenous Nonprofessional: A Strategy of Change in Community Action and Community Mental Health Programs* (New York: National Institute of Labor Education, 1964); Frank Riessman, "The Revolution in Social Work: The New Nonprofessional," *Trans-Action* II, 1 (November-December, 1964), 12-17.

19. Brager, *loc. cit.*

20. *Ibid.*, p. 40.

21. Martin L. Birnbaum and Chester H. Jones, "Activities of the Social Work Aide," *Social Casework*, XLVIII, 10 (December, 1967), 626-32.

22. *Ibid.*, p. 631.

23. Dorthea Cudaback, "Case-Sharing in the AFDC Program: The Use of Welfare Service Aides," *Social Work*, XIV, 3 (July, 1969), 93-99; Dorthea Cudaback, "Summary Report in Welfare Service Aide, and Project," Dorthea Cudaback, "Training and Education of New Careerists in Public Welfare" (Richmond: School of Social Work, University of California, 1968 and 1969, respectively, mimeographed).

24. Cudaback, "Summary Report," *op. cit.*, p. 1.

25. *Ibid.*, p. 4.

26. *Ibid.*, p. 6.

27. *Ibid.*

28. *Ibid.*, p. 1.

29. Allive del Valle and Alexander Felton, "Effects of the Project on Family Service Agencies and Urban Leagues," *Social Casework*, XLVIII, 10 (December, 1967), 636.

30. Harry Specht *et al.*, "Case Conference on Neighborhood Subprofessional Workers," *Children*, XV, 1 (January-February, 1968), 24.

31. Fred M. Loewenberg, "Social Workers and Indigenous Nonprofessionals: Some Structural Dilemmas," *Social Work*, XIII, 3 (July, 1968), 66.

32. Brager, *op. cit.*, p. 38.

33. Charles G. Grosser, "Local Residents as Mediators Between Middle-Class Professional Workers and Lower-Class Clients," *Social Service Review*, XL, 1 (March, 1966), 56-63.

34. Sherman Barr, "A Professional Takes a Second Look," *American Child*, XLIX, 1 (Winter, 1967), 14-17; Sherman Barr, *Some Observations on the Practice of Nonprofessional Workers* (New York: Mobilization for Youth, 1966).

35. Specht, *op. cit.*, p. 8.

36. Bernard Neugeboren, "New Haven's Unified Social Services Project" (New Brunswick, N.J.: Rutgers, The State University, 1968).

CHAPTER 5

Unlike education (where the professional worker, the teacher, is far more numerous than the paraprofessional), and unlike social work (where neither the professional's job is clear nor is his status secure), in health, the professional workers, that is, medical doctors, are few, and their status is secure. Something of the parameters of the health field can be seen in the changing pattern of health manpower. In 1900, for every 10 physicians, there were 6 other health personnel; in 1960, for every 10 physicians, there were 100 other health personnel. Prior to World War II, there were 2.5 times as many physicians as nurses; in 1962, there were twice as many nurses as physicians. Between 1910 and 1962, the number of physicians doubled, nurses increased sevenfold, and medical and dental technicians twentyfold.[1] In effect, the health-manpower pattern in the United States has been an increasingly smaller percentage of doctors and a rapidly increasing array of other personnel, particularly technicians, who are far below the doctor in training and education as well as skills and responsibilities. In comparison, in the Soviet Union, the ratio of physicians to nurses is 2:3, and, in addition, there are nearly as many "feldshers" (similar to our physician assistants) as physicians.[2]

Numerous studies have illustrated a misallocation of the professional's time. For example, at the VA Hospital in Grand Junction, Colorado, it was found that only "49 percent of the recorded activities were appropriate to the skills of the nursing staff."[3] At the VA Hospital in Dearborn, Michigan, 28 percent of the activities were appropriate, 18 percent clearly inappropriate, and 52 percent questionable.[4] In New York City's public schools, one third of the time of the Public Health Nurses was "used for work below the level of professional nursing skills."[5]

UPGRADING OF OLD WORKERS TO NEW JOBS

As we have indicated, nondoctors comprise the preponderant number of workers in hospitals and have done so for some time. What *is* new is that new activities are being performed, and, more significant, old workers are being upgraded to new jobs. Among some of the new job titles in a municipal hospital system for which new workers from among the poor are being trained is the obstetrical technician, who performs nearly 50 percent of the functions formerly done by a registered nurse; the unit manager, who acts as an administrative assistant in an outpatient clinic and the ward manager, who performs the same function in the wards; the chart-care technician; as well as a variety of aides and assistants in such services as radiology, anesthesiology, emergency room, and so forth.[6]

The most extensive hospital upgrading program to date was inaugurated as a joint demonstration project of the union which represented the nurses' aides (District Council 37, American Federation of State, County, and Municipal Employees) and the New York City Hospital Department. Dimensions of the three-year project, funded by the Manpower Administration, U.S. Department of Labor, are presented in Table 9.[7]

The training program involved twenty hours of work and twenty-five hours of training per week over a fourteen-month period. There were three training cycles; the first began in June, 1967, and the last ended in September, 1969. There were approximately equal numbers of trainees in their twenties, thirties, and forties. Their average grade level was 7.2 in reading and 6.5 in arithmetic; 37 percent had not completed high school.[8] An independent study of the program found the following:

> All of the graduates reported they were doing significantly different jobs than they had as nurse's aides. Over half were dispensing medicines. About a third had taken charge of wards and had supervised nurse's aides in the absence of the registered nurse normally assigned that duty. Other changes in job function included: treating sicker patients; assisting doctors with more difficult procedures, such as catheterization; writing nurse's notes and reading patient charts and reports; instructing outpatients in self-administered procedures, such as giving oneself an injection of insulin.[9]

In a comparison of these LPNs (who were trained while on the job and who had less formal schooling), with those of the regular Board of Education MDTA training program, by thirty-six supervisors and administrative personnel, twenty said they were better; fifteen, the same; and one, worse. And, in a comparison of the work of these LPNs with the graduates of the full-time School of Practical Nursing, whose admission standards include a high school diploma and tenth-grade levels of reading and mathematics, by forty-nine supervisors, four said these workers were better, thirty said they were the same, fourteen said they were worse, and one gave no response.[10]

TABLE 9

Nurses' Aide Upgrading Project, Program Statistics

Category	Percent	Number
Nurses' aides employed by the Department of Hospitals, October, 1967		7,700
Applications submitted		2,857
Entrance examinations completed		1,747
Trainees selected		
High motivation group[a] (92)		463
Trainees graduated	91[b]	
High motivation group[a] (75)	81[b]	422
Trainees licensed as LPNs	83[b]	385
High motivation group[a] (63)	64	

[a]Those participants who did not meet the regular admissions requirements but who were included in a subexperiment.

[b]Figures are in each case a percentage of the trainees selected. Actually 91 percent of the trainees graduated passed the LPN examination and were licensed as LPNs, and 83 percent of the high motivation group did so.

Source: Toward a Career Ladder in Nursing: Upgrading Nurse's Aides to LPNs Through a Work-Study Program, Final Progress Report (New York, 1970), p. 16.

NEW WORKERS FOR CHILDREN

It is in the field of pediatrics and child care that the most innovative efforts at new uses of health manpower have been made. These include the upgrading of nurses as well as bringing in new personnel. A four-month training program at the University of Colorado's Denver Medical Center produced the following:

Pediatric nurse practitioners who are able to give total care to more than 75 percent of all children who come to the field stations, including almost all of the well children (who make up slightly more than half of all the patients) as well as approximately half of the children with illnesses or injuries.

Routine checkups of infants and older children, developmental testing, various screening procedures and tests, routine immunization, complete physical examinations when indicated, as well as the management of a number of minor disorders can all be carried out by the nurse.[11]

Similar findings resulted for work in private offices, particularly as it related to well-child care, which takes up approximately half of the pediatrician's time.[12] And for sick children, the use of the nurse-practitioner allows the pediatrician to play a new role.

> In private offices, nurses can give almost complete well-child care, as well as participate in the care of the sick child. The latter may have the initial work-up by the nurse and then be seen by the physician; this allows the physician to serve as a consultant to his own patients.[13]

Both the profession and the patients (or at least their mothers; the children were not asked) approve of the use of pediatric nurse-practitioners. The following was found in a sample poll of pediatricians:

> At least two thirds of the respondents indicated that they would be willing to hire an allied health worker on a full-time or part-time basis to carry out patient-care tasks which are now predominantly performed by the pediatrician.[14]

And the profession's organized spokesman, The American Academy of Pediatrics, recommended a three-tier classification of allied health workers— pediatric nurse associate, pediatric office assistant, and pediatric aide.[15]

A survey of 145 mothers in the Seattle area found high support for the use of assistants in pediatrics. Three fourths of the mothers approved of the concept, and 94 percent said they would be willing to try it.[16] Interestingly, there was little difference in response from mothers based on the type of health care their children had been receiving—private doctors, group health facilities, or public well-baby clinics. At least 90 percent of all the mothers thought pediatric assistants could obtain blood specimens, give infant-care information, give immunization information, and interpret instructions to parents.[17] At least 80 percent thought pediatric assistants could provide normal growth and development information, take social histories, take interval developmental histories, provide telephone advice regarding routine care, and provide guidelines for growth and developmental problems.[18]

Nutritional deficiencies, especially anemia, are frequent among poor children; studies done in Boston, New York, Chicago, Washington, D.C., and Los Angeles report the incidence of iron-deficiency anemia ranging from 21 percent to 76 percent among groups of children in these cities. A Los Angeles program, funded by the Children's Bureau, sought to test whether indigenous health aides could successfully counsel parents about iron-deficiency anemia and to compare their effectiveness with that of middle-class professionals. Based on evaluation of the extent and degree of compliance with counseling instructions and their recall of nutrition information, those parents counseled by the indigenous workers performed as well or better than did those counseled by second-year medical students. The aides received 16 hours of training over a period of a week, and then spent 40 hours observing a professional dietician counsel the parents. The aides were recruited from the local Youth Opportunities Unit, and were either Black or Mexican-American, between 18 and 22 years of age. The authors of the study concluded: "Indeed, the indigenous nonprofessional may be even more effective than the professional in transmitting technical advice in a less formal manner."[19]

In an Hawaii Head Start program, indigenous paraprofessionals were used in screening tasks with 298 children, three to four and a half years old.[20] After a two-week training program, at three hours daily, the paraprofessionals conducted parent interviews (45 to 60 minutes in length) and did child screening (28 to 30 minutes). The tasks included taking the child's medical and behavioral history, completing a physical observation form, administering the Denver Developmental Screening Test, the Ammons Quick Test, and the Willoughby-Haggerty Behavior Inventory.

> Results of aides' identifications of physical problems correlated positively with findings of physical defects through traditional pediatric examination. Aides' detection of developmental problems also correlated positively with those made by psychologists.[21]

This use of indigenous paraprofessionals also characterizes many of the Maternal and Child Health Services projects. The Social Security Act of 1935 and the Amendments of 1963, 1965, and particularly 1967 (see Chapter 1) encouraged the use of aides in health- and child-care programs. A survey of 58 comprehensive health-care projects for children and youth in low-income areas, supported by the Maternal and Child Health Services, found that 53 (91%) used indigenous paraprofessional workers.[22]

In April, 1969, a study examined three of these projects (one in rural North Carolina and two in New York City) intensively. All paraprofessionals were indigenous workers and experienced homemakers. The work they did included counseling patients regarding diets, especially re newborn children; teaching food preparation; training housewives in shopping, laundering, housekeeping, baby's needs, and child care; assisting in well-baby clinics; and conducting community meetings.[23] Among the reports of supervisors was the following:

> The amount of time I spend in supervision and administration of the two aides is nominal compared to the total work they accomplish.
>
> Additional nutrition and home economics services to families enrolled in the projects were made possible through the use of aides.
>
> While behavioral changes in families cannot be wholly attributed to the nutrition and home economic services given by the aides, the professional reported that such behavior changes did occur.[24]

Examples of behavior changes included "improved homemaker skills, weight improvement of families served, greater client self-confidence, improved baby-care skills, improved health of babies, and improved consumer purchasing practices."[25]

The report concluded as follows:

[Aides] have made a contribution to the delivery of nutrition and home economics services to the families enrolled. More services were delivered . . . than would have been possible if only the professional nutritionists and home economists were employed The reasons for this include the following: The aides had time to make home visits to teach and give necessary follow-up and support; some were bilingual and could communicate with the Spanish-speaking patients more readily; they understood the culture of the patients and knew the resources available to them.[26]

RECRUITMENT, OUTREACH, AND CASEFINDING

In a Denver Maternal and Infant Care Project, "neighborhood representatives were hired specifically to represent their disadvantaged neighborhood."[27] These workers, unlike traditional health paraprofessionals, were neither closely supervised nor had tasks imposed on them. Rather, "emphasis [was] placed on the development of their unique style and relations with the population being served."[28] They performed three major roles: (a) as service expediters, they interpreted services offered to residents and also dealt with individual problems; (b) they served as neighborhood organizers; and (c) as patient representatives, they dealt with complaints, referred them to appropriate authorities, and provided necessary followup.[29]

The apparent effect of these neighborhood workers was most impressive.

Use of clinic services has shown 42 percent higher attendance during the same period of time in neighborhoods served by representatives when contrasted with neighborhoods without representatives. Four months after the establishment of a Mother and Infant Care Clinic in one neighborhood, it was determined that in excess of 60 percent of the patients had been referred by the representatives. Clinics served by representatives reported an average of 20 percent more unwed mothers than in comparable neighborhoods not served by representatives. In neighborhoods where representatives had been employed for six months or more, 50 percent of the patients are being seen in their first or second trimester. This contrasts with 32 percent in unserved neighborhoods.[30]

The importance of this outreach work is pointed out by the findings that, despite the high incidence of illness among the poor, they are serious underusers of health facilities.[31] The use of indigenous paraprofessionals in outreach work, of course, directly capitalizes on their knowledge of the local community and its knowledge of and trust in these workers. This combination

of knowledge concerning the community and the community's knowledge of
the indigenous worker is described in a New York City family planning
program.

> Efforts to introduce family planning in one neighborhood were
> totally unsuccessful until an outreach program, using only women
> indigenous to the neighborhood, was initiated. The paid paraprofes-
> sional staff, women of Puerto Rican background, were satisfied users
> of birth-control methods, recently taught by the family planning
> clinic staff; they ventured forth to visit the homes of their friends
> and neighbors in a low-income area, communicated their own
> satisfaction with family planning education, and related to the
> questions and concerns of their clients. This informal, social,
> educational model changed the neighborhood family planning
> program from an almost defunct operation to a model of successful
> service delivery in a short span of time.[32]

In describing this use of indigenous workers, Francine Sobey cited the above
(and other examples) as confirmation of Kurt Lewin's work that people learned
more readily from their peer-group than from other groups.[33]

In an Oklahoma immunization project, three public health nurses brought
in an average of 200 persons a month. However, seven indigenous
paraprofessionals who worked the same areas during the following year brought
in 2,000 persons a month. With only two and one half times as many workers,
ten times the number of people responded.[34]

In a more carefully studied project, eight Black women, all of whom were
poor, were trained to work as community health aides in a California county
health department.[35] Initially, they gathered data regarding families' immunization history, disseminated information regarding health department services,
uncovered individuals needing service, and provided family planning education.[36] The first project which suggested their special power was working with
families whose cases—involving child abuse, excessive drinking, and unsanitary
housekeeping—had been "closed" as "unreachable" by the public health nurse,
despite the continuing need of these families for help. In working with the families "over a period of four months" the indigenous workers were successful in
showing that "some progress had been made in 26 of these 30 families."[37]

Following this success, a more careful demonstration was set up as part of
a measles immunization program. "By limiting the distribution of the
information about the new vaccine to one source, the health aides, and by
observing the subsequent requests for the vaccine," the project staff felt they
could "learn more about the utility of the aide program."[38] The measles
immunization program was more complicated than other immunization efforts
in that the vaccine was to be given only to children between the ages of one
and six, not to those who had had measles, an illness easily confused with
German measles or rubella.

> Calling at every third dwelling in a mixed working-class
> neighborhood, the aides found 64 families in which there were

children who were susceptible to measles and eligible to receive the new vaccine at the clinic. Twenty-five percent of these families appeared at the next scheduled immunization clinic and requested measles vaccine; [despite other publicity efforts] there were no requests originating from other sources, either at this or at several subsequent clinics.[39]

COMMUNITY HEALTH PROGRAMS

In some of the earliest community health programs, paraprofessionals were used in efforts to bring services to those particularly difficult to reach for traditional services with largely White, middle-class personnel. In the 1950's, native aides were used at the Navaho Indian Reservation, Window Rock, Arizona, to bridge the gap between the Indians and the health services; trained natives worked with Indians and Eskimos in Canada; and former farmworkers were used to work with migrants in Florida.[40] In programs for migrant workers, indigenous aides were particularly effective. By 1966, forty-two projects funded under the Federal Migrant Health Act of 1962 had used former migrants.[41]

The largest single source of support for community health services is OEO's Comprehensive Health Services.[42] A 1967 OEO survey of paraprofessionals in Comprehensive Health Services programs found over 150 job titles—an estimated 50 of which did not exist a decade earlier.[43] One of the most innovative programs was the Montefiore Neighborhood Medical Care Demonstration in the Bronx, New York. The organization of health care revolved around a team consisting of physicians, nurses, and an indigenous family health worker. These workers were recruited from the community, and preference was given to unemployed heads of families. Among the first 28, two thirds were high school dropouts, they had an average IQ of 103, they ranged from 21 to 47 years of age, all were women, and all but 1 were married.[44] The family health workers received six months' training, most of it on the job. Their duties covered a wide program area.

The family health worker . . . has incorporated into her role some of the functions of the public health nurse, the lawyer, the social worker, the physician, and the health educator. . . . The worker's base is the health center, but much of her time is involved in making home visits in the community. . . . She is assigned from 40 to 60 families. . . . Daily activities . . . include a variety of health education, patient care, and social advocacy activities. She instructs the new mother how to bathe and feed the baby, and is alert to household hazards such as fire traps and broken paint on walls. In her training, strong emphasis is placed on patient education, case finding, the preventive aspects of medical care, and the emotional factors influencing illness.

Her patient care activities include checking blood pressure and pulse; instructing relatives of bedbound patients (bathing, skin care, changing dressings, irrigating catheters, giving enemas); carrying out the exercises prescribed by a psychiatrist; checking whether a new diabetic patient understands how to check his urine and is following his diet. She is able to collect a midstream urine and is being taught how to collect venous blood samples. In addition, she administers a check list health inventory.

During the course of her home visits, the family health worker deals with a variety of social and environmental problems. She assists a patient with heart disease to obtain a telephone through the Welfare Department, or to obtain more suitable, low-income housing for a large young family. Initiative and imagination in the family health workers are stressed as part of their patient advocacy role.

> The family health worker is trained to help people face their problems ... to listen carefully, and to think through what the patient wants to do before looking for solutions in the problem. ... To be familiar with many agencies and to evaluate which is appropriate for a particular family with a particular problem. ... To help people negotiate with agencies to get the help they need. ...[45]

Given this wide range of activities, it is not surprising "that each of the professions (e.g., lawyer, nurse, health educator, community organizer, anthropologist) looked on the newly emerging family health worker as their own subprofessional staff."[46] This tension increased as the new workers received a remarkably friendly reception in the community.

> [This was due] to her entree as a health (rather than social) worker, her status as a member of the community, and her "advocacy" role for the patient—against the establishment including, if necessary the Neighborhood Medical Care Demonstration. There has been little of the uneasiness felt by some community residents that family health workers would be used in lieu of physicians.[47]

Other New York City programs made similar use of indigenous workers. At the Harlem Hospital Center, family health workers also worked as a team with the physician and public health nurse. In a role which combined nursing, social advocacy skills, and health education, the family health workers had a caseload of twenty to forty families. Their tasks included instructing new mothers, identifying home health hazards, checking vital signs of recently released hospital patients, instructions in self-care to bedfast patients, and collecting specimens from patients.[48]

At the Martin Luther King, Jr., Health Center, a new job, the health advocate, evolved from the family health worker position. The new role included providing education and information regarding community health rights, initiating a program of environmental improvements, organizing a program of environmental improvements, organizing a program to enforce sanitation codes, developing mechanisms to secure welfare benefits for those needing special diets, instituting special programs for handicapped children, lobbying for improved recreation facilities, developing special transportation facilities for the handicapped, and developing services to meet practical needs of people in using health facilities, such as homemaker services, daycare, and transportation.[49] And, in the funding request for the Beth Israel Center to the Public Health Service, the proposal was specifically amended to include two graduates of the social health technician program to work as assistants in the Cervical Cancer Control project because of their demonstrated ability to get patients to accept services when other staff members had failed.[50]

Other new services have been offered as a result of the utilization of paraprofessional workers. A listing developed as part of an evaluation of the MFY Social Health Technician program described the following new services offered by paraprofessionals.

Bellvue Hospital Medical Social Service Program

1. Home visits for emotionally supportive purposes; and to hospitalized patients' homes prior to release to check the adequacy of conditions
2. Direct advocacy for patients
3. Accompanying groups of chronically handicapped patients on recreational outings and serving as group leaders
4. Escorting distressed patients through various hospital departments

Kings County Psychiatric Social Services

1. Researching community facilities which may be of use to patients
2. Accompanying patients in looking for housing, training, or employment
3. Conducting regular followup services to discharged patients
4. Helping discharged patients establish daily routines[51]

One aspect of community health programs, home health care, has also attracted many indigenous workers. In a report on a national demonstration project funded by OEO, the evaluators stated:

In this research study covering seven communities, respondents at every level—project personnel, physicians, nurses, and the patients themselves—are in agreement that persons from the poverty population do have the capacity to be trained to meet the need [for home health aides].[52]

They subsequently noted the following:

The reaction of the patients in all areas of the study has been overwhelmingly positive in terms of the satisfaction of the patients with the work of the aides. . . . ninety-eight percent of those reporting thus far indicate such satisfaction. Every patient interviewed stated that, given his present circumstances, he would want to have a home health aide again.[53]

ADDITIONAL STEPS

The use of paraprofessionals is not new in health and is expanding rapidly. The old paraprofessionals, nurses' aides, and the like are increasing; new workers, such as those with indigenous family health titles, are coming onto the scene, and new subdoctor roles, such as nurse-practitioners, are developing. The newest effort is the physician's assistant (PA). Since the first PA program was begun at Duke University in 1965, some forty have sprung up around the country.[54] One of the most promising is the MEDEX program in Seattle.[55] The basic idea behind this and similar programs is simple—there is a need for new health manpower to augment the physician, and in former military corpsmen and other health technicians there are pools of available resources. For the most part, the several tens of thousands of men who leave the military after having had medical training do not go into health-related work in civilian life. This is due to many factors, of course, but some of the key factors appear to be lack of transferability of the skills and training they have received, low pay for the health work which they are offered, and lack of knowledge on their part of opportunities. By providing additional civilian training for those who have had medical training and experience in the military (advanced corpsmen have had as much as 600 to 2,000 hours of formal medical training), these men are prepared for a new level of work in civilian life.

The Seattle program began in the summer of 1969, when fifteen enrollees, all former corpsmen, received three months of training at the University of Washington Medical School, followed by a year of preceptorship. They were trained in taking medical histories, conducting certain parts of a physical examination, applying and removing casts, making hospital and home rounds, assisting in surgery, and performing selected diagnostic and therapeutic procedures. Each of the fourteen who completed the training later began working for the doctors who were their preceptors.

Although the evaluation is not yet completed, the assumption of a significant number of tasks by the MEDEX has engendered unexpected enthusiasm by the physicians and nurses with whom the men work. More important, however, is the almost universal patient acceptance of this new professional.

A survey of patients showed that in 106 instances of treatment by a MEDEX, the patients rated the treatment as satisfactory as or more satisfactory than the same treatment given by a doctor.[56]

The success of this and similar programs is indicated by the fact that approximately a quarter of the money sought by the President for new health-manpower efforts in 1971 was to be used for PA programs.[57]

The use of paraprofessional personnel met with support from the profession, as well. A survey of members of the Wisconsin State Medical Society found that over 60 percent felt assistants could do work in the operating room, take histories, and perform technical procedures.[58] A like number said they felt there was a need for such personnel, and 42 percent said they would use them.[59] Those in group practice or partnership were more likely to favor use than those in solo practice, and those who were younger also were more in favor of their use.[60] In addition, professional associations and groups are also active. (See above, for discussion on the actions of the American Academy of Pediatrics in favor of a three-step hierarchy of paraprofessional positions.) In addition, as of 1970, the American Physical Therapy Association was developing an assistant category; the American Occupational Therapy Association was completely reevaluating all of its services and personnel requirements; the Academy of Orthopedic Surgeons was developing an orthopedic technical assistant position, the American Speech and Hearing Association was developing an assistant position, and the American Society of Medical Technologists was working on proficiency examinations and an educational equivalency credit system.[61]

In some areas, career-ladder programs were being mounted. The successful nurse's aide to LPN upgrading program in New York City's municipal hospitals was expanded for aides to LPN, from LPN to RN, and directly from aide to RN. And, nationally, the American Federation of State, County, and Municipal Employees Union was pushing such programs, as was the Health and Hospital Workers Union.

However, while new opportunities for the old paraprofessional were accepted, and so too was job restructuring, new career programs—both in terms of that concept's new types of work and ladders from entry level to professional—were far from being fully realized. Although the nurse's aide may now, in some few places, move while on the job to RN, or the former military corpsmen to PA, or the RN to pediatric nurse-practitioner, none of them would be any further along, if at all, to becoming a physician, than the freshman in medical school.

Health care is now the so-called big human service, both in terms of its sheer size and, more crucially, as the service now receiving priority public and political attention. The failures of Medicare and Medicaid made it obvious that more money alone would not be enough to refashion the nation's health care system. It became clear that a central part of any solution must involve new manpower. But neither the money nor the manpower itself is sufficient. As the founder of the Kaiser-Permanente system points out, what is called for is no less than a redesign of the entire health delivery system.[62] At the heart of the system proposed by Sidney R. Garfield is a health-testing and referral service which, based on the evaluation of the tests, would refer the patient for preventive maintenance, health care, or sick care. Only the sick care center would be primarily manned by medical staff (with paramedical assistance). The health testing and referral center, as well as the preventive maintenance service and the health care center would be primarily staffed by paramedical personnel (with medical supervision).[63]

New workers, trained and utilized in new ways, are the essential element if we are to develop a health care system capable of serving the needs of all of our people.

NOTES

1. *Health Manpower Perspective, 1967* (Washington, D.C.: Bureau of Health Manpower, Public Health Service, U.S. Department of Health, Education, and Welfare, 1967).

2. Victor W. Sidel, "Feldshers and 'Feldsherism,' " *New England Journal of Medicine*, CCLXXVIII, 17 (April 25, 1968), 934-39, Part I, and CCLXXVIII, 18 (May 2, 1968), 987-92, Part II, respectively.

3. Mark Haskell, *The New Careers Concept: Potential for Public Employment of the Poor* (New York: Praeger, 1969), p. 37.

4. *Ibid.*, p. 38.

5. *Ibid.*, p. 42.

6. *Ibid.*, pp. 49-51.

7. *Toward a Career Ladder in Nursing: Upgrading Nurse's Aides to LPNs Through a Work-Study Program, Final Progress Report* (New York, 1970), p. 16.

8. *Ibid., passim.*

9. *Ibid.*, p. 28.

10. *Ibid.*

11. H. K. Silver *et al.*, "Pediatric Nurse-Practitioner Program," *Journal of the American Medical Association*, CCIV, 4 (April 22, 1968), 299.

12. A. B. Bergman *et al.*, "Time-Motion Study of Practicing Pediatricians," *Pediatrics*, XXXVII, 2 (August, 1966), 254-63.

13. Silver, *loc. cit.*

14. Alfred Yankauer *et al.*, "Task Performance and Task Delegation in Pediatric Office Practice," *American Journal of Public Health*, LIX, 7 (July, 1967), 1109.

15. "Allied Health Workers in Pediatric Practice" (Chicago: American Academy of Pediatrics, 1969).

16. Patricia K. Patterson *et al.*, "Parent Reaction to the Concept of Pediatric Assistants," *Pediatrics*, XLIV, 1 (July, 1969), 75.

17. *Ibid.*, p. 72.

18. *Ibid.*, p. 73.

19. Willis A. Wingert *et al.*, "Indigenous Health Aides as Counselors to Parents About Nutrition," *Public Health Reports*, LXXXIV, 4 (April, 1969), 331.

20. Setsu Furuno and Augie Connor, "Use of Nonprofessional Personnel for Health Screening of Head Start Children," *American Journal of Orthopsychiatry*, XL, 2 (March, 1970), 300-2.

21. *Ibid.*, p. 301.

22. Helen S. Barney, "The Use of Nutrition and Home Economics Aides in Maternity and Infant Care and Children and Youth Projects," *Journal of Home Economics*, LXII, 2 (February, 1970), 114.

23. *Ibid.*, p. 115.

24. *Ibid.*, pp. 116-17.

25. *Ibid.*, p. 117.

26. *Ibid.*, p. 118.

27. James A. Kent and Harvey L. Smith, "Involving the Urban Poor in Health Services Through Accommodation—The Employment of Neighborhood Representatives," *American Journal of Public Health*, LVII, 6 (June, 1967), 998.

28. *Ibid.*

29. *Ibid.*, pp. 1000-1.

30. *Ibid.*, p. 1001.

31. I. Brightman *et al.*, "Knowledge and Utilization of Health Resources by Public Assistance Recipients," *American Journal of Public Health and the Nation's Health*, LXXIII, 10 (October, 1968), 919-25.

32. Francine Sobey, *The Nonprofessional Revolution in Mental Health* (New York: Columbia University Press, 1970), p. 152.

33. Kurt Lewin, "Forces Behind Food Habits and Methods of Change," *Bulletin of the National Research Council* (1943), p. 108.

34. James Stewart, "Employment of Indigenous Personnel as a Strategy for Increasing Immunization Rates in 'Hard Core' Areas," (Norman: University of Oklahoma, 1967), Unpub. Ph.D. Dissertation.

35. Jane Luckham and David W. Swift, "Community Health Aides in the Ghetto: The Contra Costa Project" (Richmond, Calif., unpublished manuscript, 1968).

36. *Ibid.*, pp. 6-9.

37. *Ibid.*, pp. 7-8.

38. *Ibid.*, p. 10.

39. *Ibid.*, p. 11.

40. Wilbur Hoff, "Role of the Community Health Aide in Public Health Programs," *Public Health Reports*, LXXXIV, 11 (November, 1969), 999.

41. *Ibid.*

42. Lisbeth Bamburger Schorr and Joseph T. English, "Background, Context and Significant Issues in Neighborhood Health Center Programs," *The Millbank Memorial Fund Quarterly*, XLVI, 3, Part I (July, 1968), 289-96.

43. "Manpower Development in Comprehensive Health Programs" (Washington, D.C.: Health Services Office, Office of Economic Opportunity, 1967 (mimeographed), Appendix 2.

44. Harold B. Wise *et al.*, "The Family Health Worker," *American Journal of Public Health*, LVIII, 10 (October, 1968); see also Harold B. Wise, "Montefiore Hospital Neighborhood Medical Care Demonstration," *The Millbank Memorial Fund Quarterly*, XLVI, 3, Part I (July, 1968), 297-307.

45. Wise *et al.*, *op. cit.*, pp. 1830-32.

46. *Ibid.*, p. 1833.

47. *Ibid.*, p. 1834.

48. Stella Zahn, "Neighborhood Medical Care Demonstration Training Program," *The Millbank Memorial Fund Quarterly*, XLVI, 3, Part I (July, 1968), 309-28.

49. "The Health Advocate," *Comprehensive Health Services and Career Development Technical Assistance Bulletin*, I, 6 (April, 1970), 1-8.

50. Bertram M. Beck *et al.*, *New Health Occupations Program: Report to the Office of Economic Opportunity and Proposal for a One Year Demonstration* (New York: Mobilization for Youth, 1968), p. 22.

51. "Social Health Technicians" (New York: Mobilization for Youth, 1970), pp. 2-4.

52. *Home Health Aide Demonstration: Project Evaluation* (New York: Daniel Yankelovich, Inc., 1967), p. 13.

53. *Ibid.*, pp. 17-18.

54. Some of the articles concerning the pioneering Duke program include the following: E. A. Stead, Jr., "Conserving Costly Talents—Providing Physicians' Assistants," *Journal of the American Medical Association*, XCVIII, 12 (December 5, 1966), 1108-9; E. A. Stead, Jr., "Training and Use of Paramedical Personnel," *New England Journal of Medicine*, CCLXXVII, 10 (October, 1967), 800-1; K. G. Andreoli and E. A. Stead, Jr., "Physicians' Assistants: Training Physicians' Assistants at Duke," *American Journal of Nursing*, LVII, 7 (July, 1967), 1442-43; Charles Letourneau, "The Assistant Physician," *Hospital Management*, CV, 4 (April, 1968), 55-57.
In addition, there are many articles on other programs such as the one in Colorado, at Alderson-Broaddus, in Kansas, and so forth. See H. K. Silver *et al.*, *op. cit.*; H. K. Silver *et al.*, "The Relative Roles of the Public Health Nurse and the Physician in Prenatal and Infant Supervision," *American Journal of Public Health*, LVI, 7 (July, 1966), 1097-1103; H. K. Silver, "The Pediatric Nurse Practitioner in Colorado," *The American Journal of Nursing*, LVII, 7 (July, 1967), 1442-42; E. Siegel and S. C. Bryson, "A Redefinition of the Role of the Public Health Nurse in Child Health Supervision," *American Journal of Public Health*, LIII, 7 (July, 1963), 1015-24; E. H. Townsend, "Paramedical Personnel in Pediatric Practice," *Journal of Pediatrics*, LVIII, 6 (June, 1966), 855-59; H. K. Silver, "Use of New Types of Providing Care for Children," *American Journal of Diseases of Children*, CXVI, 11 (November, 1968), 486-90; and H. C. Myers, "A New Educational Program for Physicians' Assistants," *Medical Times*, XCVII, 3 (March, 1969), 140.

55. Rodney N. Powell, "MEDEX: A Breakthrough in Medicine," *Hospital Tribune*, IV, 4 (September 21, 1970).

56. *Ibid.*

57. *New York Times*, February 19, 1971, p. 1.

58. Robert D. Coye and Marc F. Hansen, "The 'Doctor's Assistant,' " *Journal of the American Medical Association*, CCIX, 4 (July 28, 1969), Table I.

59. *Ibid.*, p. 530.

60. *Ibid.*, Table III.

61. Israel Light, "Development and Growth of New Allied Health Fields," *Journal of the American Medical Association*, CCX, 1 (October 6, 1969), 120.

62. Sidney R. Garfield, "The Delivery of Medical Care," *Scientific American*, CCXXII, 4 (April, 1970), 15-23.

63. *Ibid.*, p. 22.

6

POLICE,
CORRECTIONS,
AND
LAW ENFORCEMENT

The term, "paraprofessional," in police and corrections work is, in a sense, a misnomer for few of the professionals possess college degrees, the usual, if often irrelevant, denominator of the class. More distinguishing, especially in police work, is indigeneity, although professional status is also a factor in parole and probation work, and, of course, in legal services.

A number of recent surveys concluded that police departments were understaffed. A 1967 survey reported that large-city forces averaged 10 percent under authorized strength. In a 1969 survey of 39 cities with populations between 300,000 and 1 million, police departments averaged 7 percent below authorized strength.[1] A series of national bodies noted the underrepresentation of minority-group members on police forces; these studies include the President's Commission on Law Enforcement and Administration (1967), the National Advisory Commission on Civil Disorders (1968), the Commission on the Causes and Prevention of Violence (1969), and the U.S. Civil Rights Commission (1970).

In corrections, a Presidential Commission estimated a need for personnel to be increased 2.5 times by 1975. It especially emphasized the need for new types of personnel required by new types of correctional institutions, those with a rehabilitation emphasis and which are community based, the increased use of probation, and halfway houses.[2] And the Joint Commission on Correctional Manpower and Training (1969) not only placed special emphasis on the role of minority staff but also made recommendations to further career-ladder programs, including the elimination of formal tests, expansion of two-year college programs, increased use of former offenders, and the development of programs to train trainers.[3]

Similar developments have taken place in legal services programs. In 1967, a Presidential Commission recommended the use of persons who were not members of the bar. A 1968 meeting of the American Assembly on Law and a Changing Society recommended the employment of subprofessionals and paraprofessionals. And in 1968, an American Bar Association annual convention resolution "recognized that there are many tasks in serving clients' needs which can be performed by a trained nonlawyer and assistants working under the direction and supervision of a lawyer."[4]

A 1969 survey of New Careers programs found approximately 6 percent of the participants placed in law enforcement and public safety agencies.[5] Among the agencies were 28 police and sheriffs' departments, usually in smaller departments with a few placements; 26 correctional agencies, many with large numbers of placements (e.g., the Ohio Youth Commission, with 160 enrollees, and the Los Angeles Probation Department, with 98 enrollees); 6 court agencies; and 2 legal-aide societies. Something of the range of these activities can be seen in the unusually varied placements in San Diego—City Sheriff's Department, County Honor Camp, County Probation Department, State Department of Corrections, State Youth Authority, and City Police Department.[6]

LAW ENFORCEMENT

A Richmond, California, program in the mid-1960's used indigenous workers in police-community relations.[7] A Citizens Review Committee Report, in evaluating the program, stated:

> The Police Department staff feels that they are now able to help many families which they had not been otherwise able to help. In several cases, Juvenile Bureau patrolmen have requested the assistance of aides. The services provided by the aides give many families the feeling that the city really does care about them and wants to help them.[8]

And the Committee noted: "A strongly affirmative response was also elicited by a questionnaire to recipients of the Police-Community Aide services as part of evaluating the program."[9]

New Haven, Connecticut, built on an unsuccessful New Careers program; given low screening standards, the department was unable to supply the necessary remedial education, supervision, and supportive services. A new program was then instituted, with state funds. The aides worked at three levels: For the first six months, they worked out of neighborhood centers concerned with youth problems; during the second six months, they rotated through various departmental units; and during the second year, their work emphasized law-enforcement activities.[10]

The Compton, California, department established a community service officer (CSO) position with civil service status and a career-ladder to regular police positions. The objectives of the program included "improvement of police service in high-crime areas, relief of police officers from lesser duties, improvement of relations with minority groups, and increasing the number of minority officers on the police force."[11] The CSO program of the Justice Department's Law Enforcement Assistance Agency was providing funds to double the number of slots; Chicago had 400, and programs were being developed in Brooklyn, New York, Winston-Salem, North Carolina, and Baltimore, Maryland.

After the Watts riots of 1965, the Los Angeles Police Department began a program of using indigenous workers; all were school dropouts, and 75 percent were convicted felons. Activities in which they were engaged included school visitations, training of teachers, supervision of youth events, operating a summer youth program and a summer camp, and speaking at community and parent-teachers' association meetings. Within the Police Department, they worked in the Crime and Narcotic Prevention units and in the Police Academy's training program.[12]

COURT PROGRAMS

There have also been various court programs. The Manhattan Court Employment Project (MCEP) was designed for the following:

to intervene in the usual court process just after a defendant's arrest, to offer him counseling and job opportunities and, if he cooperates and appears to show promise of permanent change, to recommend that the prosecutor and the judge dismiss the charges against him without ever deciding whether he is guilty.[13]

The key project workers were paraprofessional exoffenders used as counselors (called reps). Their activities included interviewing prospective participants, carrying case responsibilities, making referrals, conducting group-counseling sessions, keeping records, carrying out liaison activities with the project's Career Development Unit, and appearing in court to make recommendations as to case disposition.[14] The reps had prior prison records from 2 years and six months to 19 years. Their effectiveness lay in the following:

they speak the language of the streets, know the ghetto neighborhoods, and are themselves extraordinary examples of people once in the same circumstances as the participants but who are now visibly making it in, instead of outside, the system.[15]

In the first 23 months, the project handled 850 participants. As a result of the intercession, 343 were employed, 29 were in training, and 51 were students; 427 were either unemployed or no information was available. In summarizing the reps' role, the Project Director stated:

The reps are capable of establishing a relationship of respect, trust, often affection with significant numbers of participants. The main reason is their commitment to each participant, independent of stereotype or even, frequently, the participants' past behavior. The reps have consistently assumed a partisan role for their participants in the face of the court, the prosecutor, and MCEP administrators. For example, they will continue to work with the addict even though they have failed to persuade 90 percent of the previous addicts to seek treatment or remain in the program.[16]

Interestingly, the reps had better results when they were assigned to meet with the participants in their committees.[17]

A similar program, Project Crossroads, operated in the Juvenile and General Sessions Courts of Washington, D.C., between January 15, 1968, and February 1, 1971.[18] From April, 1968, through September, 1970, 825 young offenders were enrolled in the project: "Charges against 467 enrollees had been dropped due to their successful project participation, while 283 were returned to normal court processing, primarily because of unsatisfactory program performance."[19] In a number of ways, the project results are impressive.

> The employment rate among former adult enrollees a year after leaving the project was double their employment rate at enrollment, and this despite the fact that almost none were in their Crossroads-obtained jobs a year later.[20]

Furthermore, the project results showed the following:

> The recidivism rate of participants was less than half that of those for a control group consisting of a similar population of adult first offenders who did not receive project services. It was also 44 percent lower than for those controls who had their charges dismissed in the normal court processing, and a third lower for *all* former participants—favorable and unfavorable—than for the control group as a whole.[21]

As was the case with MCEP, the use of paraprofessional personnel, including former offenders, was a key feature of the program. The project report noted:

> such personnel have been found to be very effective but it is a fallacy to assume that *any* indigenous, noncredentialed worker can perform at a high level of proficiency without training or supervision.[22]

In a special program evaluation, Roberta Rooner-Pieczenic reported:

> The positive role model offered the participant by the staff, as interpreted by the participant evaluation forms, leads this researcher to believe that the "new careers" person's value to the program cannot be overestimated.[23]

CORRECTIONS

One of the most successful new careers programs was that conducted by J. Douglas Grant in the California Men's Prison.[24] The program was unique in that it was conducted in a prison, and that the participants (prisoners) were trained not to work in a particular service area but as general new careers program developers and trainers. The eighteen participants, half of whom had been convicted of armed robbery, went on to play key leadership roles in new careers programs throughout the country, and four years later, only one had been reconfined. One of the participants was the organizer of the National Association of New Careerists; another was its president; a third became the director of a California new careers program. A fourth became a senior trainer in several antipoverty programs and was the organizer of the citywide Los Angeles New Careers Organization (LANCO), and a fifth held the number-two position in the Youth Services Office of the Department of Health, Education, and Welfare. A survey of corrections programs reported that "these studies reached the same conclusion: The impact of the nonprofessional on the inmate is greater than that of the professional."[25]

The New York State Division of Youth began using exoffenders in a variety of programs in the 1950's. The California State Department of Corrections, Parole, and Community Services used indigenous workers as parole aides and research aides. And in Seattle, exoffenders, themselves still on parole, were used for the following:

> [to] interview parolees, counsel them, make preparole job placement investigations, complete progress reports, aid in investigation of parole violations, make recommendations re sending parolees back to prison, [and] help parolees get jobs and needed training.[26]

One of the most innovative programs was conducted by the Los Angeles County Probation Department. Initially, a few aides were placed as part of the antipoverty program in September, 1965. Since then, well over 300 paraprofessionals have worked in the department. As of 1970, 131 community-worker positions were authorized in the department. In July, 1969, a three-step ladder was established—"Community Worker I, II, and III." Many of those in the latter two grades were in the Reeducation of Delinquency Through Expansion of Opportunity (RODEO) program, an innovative and rapidly expanding community treatment program for seriously delinquent youth who would otherwise be removed from their homes and communities. One of the key elements in RODEO was the sharing of responsibility for providing probation services by a team consisting of one professional probation officer and two community workers.

In testifying before the Senate Manpower Subcommittee, the county's personnel director focused on the key role of the indigenous workers and the dramatic effect in terms of service quality.

> The results after the first year of experimentation . . . indicated that this approach [the use of indigenous workers in RODEO] was successful in all respects. It was determined that in controlling recidivism patterns normally expected of juvenile offenders and in reestablishing the juvenile with the positive institutions of society, school, employment, etc., this approach was more successful than either the camps program or the traditional support methods.[27]

Although not as elaborate as the RODEO program, programs in Milwaukee and New York also reported impressive results. In Milwaukee, in a program operated by the Commandoes, a militant community group, former offenders worked with parolees and probationers. The parole revocation rate for those youth served by the program was 25 percent as compared with a statewide average of 50 percent.[28] And in New York City, in a program operated by the HARYOU-Act, an antipoverty program, which also used exoffenders, 75 percent of those released through it were not rearrested; this was three times the general rate.[29]

LEGAL SERVICES

The largest use of paraprofessionals in legal services was in the OEO-funded Legal Services Program, where over 800 programs used paraprofessionals.[30] The Legal Unit of MFY also used paraprofessionals in juvenile and domestic relations cases.[31] One of the more elaborate programs was that of the Dixwell Legal Rights Association which not only operated its own legal service program but also trained workers for other New Haven, Connecticut, agencies, such as the schools, urban-renewal programs, hospitals, the welfare department, and OEO's-Legal Services Programs across the country. The Dixwell workers acted as negotiators, intermediaries, and advocates. An evaluation study reported: "The lay workers have been able to satisfactorily settle more than 80 percent of the cases they have handled."[32] And in an interesting training consortium, the College of Human Services and the Columbia University Law School were training indigenous workers who were assigned to Legal Services and Legal Aid Society programs in metropolitan New York.

Furthermore, the use of paraprofessionals in law was not limited to public sector programs. A Great Bend, Kansas, law firm, specializing in accident cases, employed twenty-three lay assistants and three lawyers. And a Boston firm employed a score of paraprofessionals to assist its hundred or so lawyers.[33] Indicative of the prospects in this area was the establishment of a private training school, the Paraprofessional Institute, in Philadelphia, which recently graduated its first class; all of its members were placed with private law firms.

And, as part of his proposal to reform the court system, President Nixon proposed that many of the routine tasks done by judges be taken over by nonlawyer "para-judges," to give the judges more time to judge.[34]

CONCLUSION

There have been many problems in using indigenous workers in the area of police, safety, and corrections programs. Neither the organization, previous history, nor bent of their regular personnel was likely to predispose such agencies to the special efforts necessary to initiate and make successful such programs. Also, the often menial and boring tasks and ill-defined roles for the workers posed a particular problem. And, particularly in police work, paraprofessionals faced antagonism from members of the department as a fifth column from the community, and from community members as "junior pigs." Also, the drive to professionalize these agencies, usually a synonym for raising the educational level of the entrance requirements and recruitment of community people without formal degrees and often with criminal records, presented additional obstacles.

The fact that successes such as those described here as well as many others have occurred is a tribute to the power of the paraprofessionals, the effect of their work, and the boldness of some innovative agencies.

NOTES

1. Cited in Arnold Trebach and Evelyn Idelson, *New Careers in Justice: A Status Report* (Washington, D.C.: National Institute for New Careers, 1970), p. 3.

2. *Ibid.,* p. 5.

3. *Ibid.,* pp. 5-6.

4. *Ibid.,* p. 7.

5. National Institute for New Careers, *An Assessment of Technical Assistance and Training Needs in New Careers Projects Being Sponsored by the United States Training and Employment Service, Manpower Administration, U.S. Department of Labor* (Washington, D.C.: University Research Corporation, 1969).

6. Trebach and Idelson, *op. cit.,* p. 10.

7. Lisa Liebert, "Police-Community Relations and The Role of The Nonprofessional" (New York: New Careers Development Center, New York University, 1968), pp. 12-14.

8. *Ibid.,* p. 13.

9. *Ibid.*

10. Trebach and Idelson, *op. cit.,* pp. 15-16.

11. *Ibid.,* p. 17.

12. "An Interium Evaluation of the Community Relations Aides' Performance in the Community Relations Program" (Los Angeles: Los Angeles Police Department, 1969).

13. *The Manhattan Court Employment Project of The Vera Institute of Justice, Summary Report on Phase One: November 1, 1967 to October 3, 1969* (New York: Vera Institute of Justice, 1970), p. 7.

14. Vera Institute of Justice, *The Manhattan Court Employment Project, Phase I* (New York, 1970).

15. *The Manhattan Court, op. cit.,* p. 27.

16. *Ibid.*

17. *Ibid.,* p. 29.

18. Leon G. Lieberg, *Project Crossroads: A Final Report to the Manpower Administration, U.S. Department of Labor* (Washington, D.C.: National Committee on Children and Youth, 1971).

19. *Ibid.,* p. 4.

20. *Ibid.,* p. 5.

21. *Ibid.*

22. *Ibid.,* p. 8.

23. Roberta Rooner-Pieczenic, *Project Crossroads as Pre-Trial Intervention: A Program Evaluation* (Washington, D.C.: National Committee for Children and Youth, 1970), p. 37.

24. J. Douglas Grant, "The Offender as a Correctional Manpower Resource," in Frank Riessman and Hermine I. Popper, *Up From Poverty: New Career Ladders for Nonprofessionals* (New York: Harper and Row, 1968).

25. Judith G. Benjamin *et al., Pros and Cons: New Roles for Nonprofessionals in Corrections* (Washington, D.C.: Office of Juvenile Delinquency and Youth Development, U.S. Department of Health, Education, and Welfare, 1966), p. 13.

26. Trebach and Idelson, *op. cit.,* p. 21.

27. Gordon Nestig, "Testimony Presented Before The U.S. Senate Labor Committee, Sub-Committee on Manpower," Los Angeles, January 7, 1970.

28. *New Careers Newsletter,* II, 6 (Winter, 1968) p. 5.

29. *Amsterdam News,* April 20, 1969.

30. Richardson White, Jr. and John H. Stein, *Paraprofessionals in Legal Services Programs: A Feasiblity Study* (Washington, D.C.: National Institute for Justice and Law Enforcement, 1968).

31. Trebach and Idelson, *op. cit.*, p. 24.

32. *Ibid.*

33. White and Stein, *op. cit.*, pp. 71-78.

34. *New York Times*, March 12, 1971, p. 1.

7

Thus far, we have examined but one facet of the paraprofessional effort. While the effect of paraprofessionals on education, mental health, social service, health, and police and correction practice may be the point at which their work must ultimately be justified, the paraprofessional effort has many other ramifications which are of interest in terms of their effect on services as well as in and of themselves. It is to these issues that we now turn: the effect of participation on the paraprofessional worker himself (or, more generally, herself); the effect on the professionals with whom paraprofessionals work, the agencies which employ them, and the unions which are increasingly organizing them; the development of career-advancement programs for paraprofessionals; the effects on colleges and related training issues; the costs and potential economic benefits; and critical evaluations. Finally, we will summarize earlier material and suggest some future directions.

EFFECTS ON THE PARAPROFESSIONAL*

Perhaps the simplest statement of effects on paraprofessionals came from a critic, Charles G. Grosser, who noted that the employment of the paraprofessional "has profound consequences for the nonprofessionals themselves", including their standard of living and continued education and training.[1] A report on the Richmond, California, program contained a more expanded picture.

The program resulted in increased knowledge about the community and citizenship participation, development of personal skills and

---

*Effects as related to education, training, and career development are discussed in a separate section, below.

potential, changes in social and political outlook, and transformation of personal identity.

The consequence of finding a line of work in which one is competent and that gets rewarded socially is a clearer concept of who one is, of what is one's place in the world. The work of providing social services and the emerging role of community spokesman had these identity effects for many of the Richmond workers who did not previously have an occupational and community role or clearcut notion of their social function. . . . Previous moods of apathy and discouragement were replaced by productive activism and high morale.[2]

The exhaustive study of the Minneapolis New Careers program reported similar effects on the paraprofessional's sense of self.

[There are] significant changes in the self-concept of these individuals as they participate in the New Careers Program, and, by and large, one could establish that these changes have been in a favorable direction in terms of the way the person thinks of himself. Self-conception has been elevated.[3]

A second key finding of the Minneapolis program was that, although for some of the participants the program initially was "just a job," they became increasingly concerned with and devoted to human service work.[4] Unfortunately, however, it was all too common to find, for the paraprofessional, that the "satisfactions which accrue from performing helpful, socially useful work have initially had to compensate for the low salaries and uncertain futures of these jobs."[5]

The Minneapolis group also studied a sample of 105 individuals who left the New Careers program there. They found significant demographic differences between those who left and those who stayed. Over-all, men were more likely to leave than women, younger persons than older ones, non-Whites more so than Whites, separated or divorced persons than married ones.[6] Explanatory data were less complete than demographic data. Some suggestions may be in order, however. It seems that the key factor in the greater proportion of men leaving had to do with the inadequacy of salary. As for a disproportionate number of younger workers leaving, for many, at least, the New Careers program was useful in getting them a step into (and up) the human services work world. Many obtained the GED, and they then went on to better employment on their own. There appears to be no general explanation for the racial difference. As to the greater retention of married persons, this appears to be a part of the pattern wherein the program had the greatest holding power for the older, married women.

Another aspect where program stayins differed from dropouts was the latter's more professional orientation.

They [the dropouts] feel more strongly than the stayins that semiprofessional qualifications are necessary for a New Careerist;

they seem to be more separated, at least mentally, from the low-income community; and they have a self-image which more often includes the idea that they are professional workers than is the case with the stayins.[7]

From the very first discussions of indigenous paraprofessionals, this question of the worker's professionalization has been raised. Many, such as Arthur Pearl and Frank Riessman, warned of the danger and pointed out problems to be avoided, including training by professionals, "increased general association with professionals in the agency," "being given status and recognition by the agency and thereby acquiring some identification with professional models," and "searching for a career line."[8] However, few have developed any hard data as to what actually happens to the indigenous worker.

The Minneapolis group sought to ascertain whether the paraprofessional became "contaminated" by professionalization. They counterposed a "community orientation", which incorporated a feeling of oneness with the people of the poverty neighborhoods, a rejection of the professional as the one who could provide the solutions to the problems of poor people, and a sense that the poor were the only ones who really knew about poverty, with a "professional orientation," where the individual felt that he was different from those of the low-income neighborhood and had respect for the professional's training and knowledge.[9] The participants entering the Minneapolis program already had strong "community orientation," and the study examined changes over a fifteen-month period.[10] Six statements were used to measure the participants' orientation.

It was necessary to be a semiprofessional in order to be effective. "There was an across-the-board change toward more community orientation attitudes. And this took place on an item that already showed heavy community-orientation response."[11]

Aides are the most concerned people in the neighborhood. "In sum, on this item . . . which basically reflects New Careerists' relationship to their own community, they have become more professionally oriented."[12]

Aides are usually different from most poverty area residents. The aides begin very community oriented on this item and largely stay that way. The aide's feeling of being *like* his fellow poverty resident goes through some changes early in his involvement with New Careers, but whatever the changes are, they are nullified over the long run.[13]

Aides have more understanding of poverty than professionals. "Every subgroup, as well as the group as a whole, became more community oriented on this item over the fifteen month period."

"This is perhaps the most distinctive shift in role orientation in the data. . . . [Even] though New Careerists have had fifteen months of experience working with professionals, they feel less confident of the professional's qualifications to deal with the problems of poverty."[14]

I consider myself a professional worker. Generally there was no change in the initially community orientation rating on the item over the period.[15]

I would like to be a supervisor. "The basic trend over the fifteen-month period is a change toward greater community orientation."[16]

In sum, New Careerists have become more community oriented on four items, more professionally oriented on one, and have experienced no change in one item. In short, the basic trend has been toward increasing community orientation.[17]

And the one item when they move in the direction of "professional orientation" emphasized their own individual, special qualities as contrasted with separating themselves from the community. It seems that as these indigenous workers became more familiar with professional performance and practice, they grew to have more doubts about it and to become strengthened in their allegiance to the community, its strengths, and processes of goal achievement. It may be, then, that the usual dichotomization between service programs and social-action techniques may not be as sharp as it is usually presented. "The data seem to say that New Careerists are succeeding as paraprofessionals, but that they are doing it within the modes of action and expression that they have as members of low-income groups."[18]

Not only does it seem that paraprofessionals are not being contaminated by professionals, but taking from the world of the professional while keeping their own community orientation, they are also assuming new leadership positions in community-based institutions. For example, in the three school districts in New York City where "demonstration" community control projects took place (Intermediate School 201, Ocean Hill-Brownsville, and Two Bridges) and where indigenous workers were heavily used, 44 percent of the members of the elected governing board under the city's new school-decentralization program were paraprofessionals and antipoverty program employees, as compared to only 5 percent for the city's schools as a whole.[19]

PARAPROFESSIONALS, PROFESSIONALS, AND THE AGENCIES

Grosser provided evidence of the effect of paraprofessionals on the professionals with whom they worked in various federal manpower programs: "Not only is the presence of nonprofessionals very much felt by neighborhood populations but they also affect professional practices in these agencies."[20] In looking at the effect on state employment services offices of the employment of paraprofessionals, he noted:

[Their employment] forces the agency to a degree of accountability to the client community [which] is contrary to the traditional pattern in all service agencies of professional self-regulation and accountability to the total community and to the employment service's view of its responsibility to the employer.[21]

Unlike the traditional focus which has been to meet the needs of employers, paraprofessionals "often alienate employers; they tend to demand rather than ask for job placements."[22]

Grosser remarked on the contrast between what may have been the agency's intent in instituting a paraprofessional program and the actual consequence.

The introduction of a program device as innovative as this one, even if the original intention is only to improve services, must soon produce strains leading to alterations in patterns of agency function.[23]

Not only did the introduction of the paraprofessional directly affect the service, it also affected the professional and the agency. Grosser went further and also suggested: "Professionals in these projects are more effective with the poor than their counterparts in ongoing agencies.[24]

The effect has not been limited to individual agencies. At the national level, in addition to the funding of new careers programs by the Labor Department, large grants have been made by OEO, the Department of Housing and Urban Development (HUD), and the various operating agencies of the Department of Health, Education, and Welfare (HEW). There have been smaller grant efforts at the departments of Justice and Commerce. HEW has sought to provide a departmentwide impact through the establishment of an Office of New Careers in the Secretary's office. In commenting on the establishment of the Office of New Careers, July 10, 1969, Under-Secretary John Veneman said the following to a departmentwide meeting:

The Secretary is firmly committed to the new careers concept—to bringing new people into jobs and careers, to enabling human service agencies more effectively to provide health, education, and welfare services to all Americans. We believe that the Office of New Careers can and will make a major contribution toward these ends. The support and backing of the Secretary is here. In concert and cooperation with the people of the operating agencies, I know that the Office of New Careers will make a major stamp upon the work and activities of the Department.[25]

And in a foreward to the Office's first publication, Assistant Secretary James Farmer, who sparked the establishment of the new Office, quoted Secretary Robert Finch.

From the very first days of my tenure at HEW I have been totally committed to the increased training and use of paraprofessionals—

"new professionals"—in teaching, in health services, in social services of every category. There simply are no real solutions in any of these areas of concern without new and newly trained manpower.

Beyond the desire to equip people with needed skills and to put them to work, my concern is with the delivery of effective human services—and experience is showing that paraprofessionals are contributing to better services all across the board.[26]

In California, a statewide new careers program began by executive order of the governor in 1968.[27] In that year, 583 positions in 8 classifications were initially identified as suitable for entry-level workers. A year later, 1,190 jobs in 22 classifications were included. Not only were classifications identified for inclusion in new categories, but civil service changes were under way. At the national level, the National Civil Service League has been a supporter of new careers programs and testified before Congress in favor of the government as employer of the first resort.[28] It also supported the publishing of material.[29] Additionally, it supported the provision of technical assistance to local programs including Model Cities agencies on how to master the civil service system.[30]

Many individual states have taken steps to adjust their own regulations.[31] In California, primary attention has been given to a four-step ladder in social services. The entry position, which pays $415 a month, has no formal education requirements and is seen as essentially a training slot. After six months of satisfactory work and passage of an oral examination, a person can move to the next step, social service assistant I. This is a permanent civil service class with pay beginning at $480 a month. There are two further paraprofessional positions—social service assistant II and then counselor associate. Movement to the top of this ladder (at a monthly salary of over $700) can be based on work experience only, or a combination of work and education. However, entrance into the first professional level, intake counselor, does require academic training. Each rung of the social service ladder has two classes—one for English-speaking and the other for Spanish-speaking employees.

In less than a year, 441 job-class specifications were revised with respect to minimum education or experience requirements by the Illinois Civil Service Commission. These classes represented over 65 percent of the positions in the state civil service. Job-class series in child care, prisons, and youth programs no longer required any formal education or work experience prior to hiring.

In Michigan, 55 new careerists were employed in 4 state departments. Following a six month probationary period at $1.94 an hour, 40 workers moved to the second step at $2.40 an hour. Although the workers received the same fringe benefits as other civil service employees from the first day of their employment, they could not attain full civil service status until the end of the two-year program, upon passage of an examination.

And in New Jersey, a new job series was introduced in the drug-prevention field. Unique is the existence of dual entry level positions—one for former addicts just coming off drugs and the other for those who have been "clean."

Another index of growing institutionalization of paraprofessional programs is the support for them with local funds, moving from the exclusive reliance on federal sources. As noted in Chapter 2, an NEA survey of 799 school districts across the country found that 18 percent of the paraprofessional programs were funded through state and local funds alone. And a 1970 study, conducted by the Ohio Education Association, reported that 55 percent of the paraprofessional programs in the state were supported by state and/or local funds; 25 percent by state, local, and federal funds; and fewer than 20 percent by federal funds alone.[32]

PROFESSIONAL ORGANIZATIONS AND UNIONS

Professional organizations have responded to paraprofessional programs in a number of ways. As described in Chapter 1, various social work groups addressed issues relating to paraprofessionals in the early 1960's. In 1968, a joint report of the National Association of Social Workers (NASW) and the Council of Social Work Education (CWSE) endorsed the concept of new careers as an important new manpower resource, and recognized "the inclusion of personnel indigenous to the client system as part of social work manpower."[33] The report went on to recommend that jobs be developed with tasks stemming from the needs of clients rather than from those which social workers do not want to do; that there be vertical and horizontal mobility; that education for career advancement be provided; that a team concept of service be developed; and that training be provided for professionals in how to better work with paraprofessionals.[34] CWSE also moved away from its traditional (sole) concern with master's degree programs and developed guidelines for two-year community and social services college programs.[35] It also held a series of regional workshops to promote such programs.

The American Public Welfare Association (APWA) has also been a strong supporter of the use of paraprofessionals. It devoted a special issue of its journal to these programs and conducted regional workshops and training programs for local welfare officials. In December, 1969, APWA endorsed paraprofessional programs, with the proviso that such programs must include released time for education, must provide for education leading to college degrees, and must include career ladders.[36] Unfortunately, NASW's considerable support for the use of paraprofessionals has not included their admission as full voting members in the organization.[37]

Various health organizations have taken actions regarding paraprofessionals and paraprofessional programs. In 1969, the American Public Health Association (APHA) granted Conference status to a group called the New Professional Health Workers, a paraprofessional organization with its base in Philadelphia and Pittsburgh and affiliates elsewhere. In 1970, the APHA convention carried recognition of the group further by assigning a staff member to work with it toward acceptance in 1971 as a full Section of APHA.[38] This rapid progress is in marked contrast to the usual four to eight years to move from Conference to Section. And the American Orthopsychiatric Association voted by membership referendum to admit those, including paraprofessionals, who lacked a master's degree but presented equivalent work experience.[39]

The American Medical Association's House of Delegates, in December, 1969, endorsed two avenues to advancement in new health occupations. In addition to the traditional route of academic preparation and training, they supported "Advancement through practical experience and attainment of a high level of competence."[40]

Similarly, as was true of NASW, the largest professional education association, NEA, encouraged paraprofessional programs, but NEA has thus far limited the paraprofessionals' participation in their organization.[41] However, NEA's competitor in organizing public school personnel, the American Federation of Teachers (AFT), has been both a supporter of paraprofessional programs and actively recruited paraprofessionals as full members of their locals. At the national level, AFT organizers have assisted locals in organizing of paraprofessionals, and its twenty-twenty plan—teachers to teach no more than 20 pupils at a time, 20 hours per four-day week—involves use of paraprofessionals on the fifth day. AFT locals in dozens of cities have organized paraprofessionals, often winning contracts which include both traditional "bread and butter" gains as well as the special career concerns of paraprofessionals. This combination is illustrated in the contract won by AFT's New York City local, the United Federation of Teachers (UFT). Over 4,000 aides who work in the classroom from kindergarten through second grade are covered in a new contract with starting salaries for entry workers at $2.50 an hour and at $5.05 for those at the top of the paraprofessional ladder (a 140% increase over the life of the three-year contract); a guarantee of 42 weeks of work plus a four-week vacation; a college-career program; and full fringe benefits.[42] The union has just won bargaining rights to represent the additional 6,000 classroom aides in grades three through twelve.

District Council 37, American Federation of State, County, and Municipal Employees (AFSCME), has not only won the same contract as the UFT for its members who work for the Board of Education as family and community workers, but has made career development a central part of its organizing and bargaining strategy. In 1967, in a bargaining election with the Teamsters to win the right to represent workers in the municipal hospitals of New York City, District Council 37 made the achievement of an upgrading plan a central part of its campaign and, when it won, attributed a major portion of the reason for its victory to the career-development plank in its campaign. The nurse's aide to LPN upgrading program described in Chapter 5 is a fulfillment of that campaign. Since that initial program, Council 37 has pushed further for additional upgrading programs. And AFSCME has operated upgrading programs for hospital workers in Boston, Cleveland, and Minneapolis.

In the voluntary hospital field, the National Union of Hospital Workers has built on the upgrading work of its founding local, New York City's Local 1199. Organizing is going on in Baltimore, Charleston, Dayton, Durham, Philadelphia, Pittsburgh, and Washington, D.C. The contract won by 1199, which provides for a fund of 1 percent of total payroll for training and upgrading, is the standard for other cities.

The participation of these and other unions has brought the concepts of new careers programs—particularly as they relate to career ladders and built-in education and training—to the old paraprofessionals such as the some 400,000 nurses' aides or nearly 100,000 psychiatric aides. Thus, the benefits which were provided to new paraprofessionals from the community through federal programs are being sought and won for their old members by the unions, who are also organizing these new workers.

TRAINING, EDUCATION, AND UPGRADING

From the earliest formulations in the 1960's, advocates of the use of indigenous paraprofessionals were concerned with upward mobility for the participants—not merely a job, but a career. (Programs using what we labeled "new nonprofessionals" in Chapter 3, that is, those with formal education but lacking professional training, have been less concerned about careers.) In reporting on one of the first programs, that in the California Men's Prison, Joan Grant wrote, "within a year the gratefulness of the aides for the job vanishes and demands for upgrading, training, and definition of career lines begin to be made."[43] The participants in this program have gone on to impressive positions in new careers and other social welfare programs at an average salary considerably in excess of $10,000 a year.

A review of the Scheuer Amendment New Careers programs, three years after they began, stated:

Even though career ladders have been worked out and approved by agency executives, in many projects they still have not been built into the job structure, and service and personnel system, staffing pattern and budget planning of the potential employing agencies.[44]

A study conducted by the New Careers Training Laboratory of community action agencies across the country found that nearly one fifth of the professional positions in these agencies were held by persons who had come into their agencies as paraprofessionals.[45] And in the Head Start program, there is an agencywide mandate for career development which includes local Career Development Committees, individual career advancement programs, as well as college training (discussed below).

The Office of Education's new Career Opportunities Program involves over 8,000 paraprofessionals in the public schools of some 132 communities around the country. Pertinent features of this program include the emphasis on rapid movement toward a degree (four to five years for a person with or without a high school diploma) and a teaching license while working as a paraprofessional; bringing people into the program at various rungs on the career ladder, depending on their previous education and experience and present skills and knowledge; and the inclusion of a significant number of male paraprofessionals as a result of the program's requirement that 40 percent of the participants be veterans from the Vietnam war.

We have already noted the large paraprofessional programs in the schools and hospitals of New York City. In the former, contracts won by the two unions provided for a career-ladder program and paid released time from work for attendance at college (also employer paid) for the approximately 6,000 members of the present bargaining units. And negotiations were also underway to include an additional 6,000 school workers under the contract.

In the hospitals, nearly 500 nurses' aides became LPNs as a result of an upgrading program, and plans of the new Health and Hospital Corporation, sparked by the interest of AFSCME District Council 37, included such upgrading programs as aide to LPN, LPN to RN, aide to technician, and aide to RN, all designed to allow the worker to remain employed and continue to be paid while being trained.

In 1965-66, 118 paraprofessionals were trained in 6 twelve-week cycles to work at 34 New York City social welfare agencies.[46] In 1969, 83 of these were located and 26 were intensively interviewed. At the time of the followup study, some three to four years after the initial training, 24 of the 26 were employed at 8 different social service agencies; 20 worked for the original agency which had employed them following the training.[47] The starting salary for the group had averaged $4,534 and ranged from $3,000 to $6,000. At the time of the followup, salaries averaged $6,773, a nearly 50 percent increase, and ranged from $5,150 to $10,300.[48] However, while the paraprofessionals' work history and salary levels have improved markedly, their lack of at least a baccalaureate degree meant that further advancement was blocked. A report on the study noted the high quality of the paraprofessionals' work, and personal salary gains, and concluded:

But "most relevant," according to the report, is the finding that "opportunities for genuine career advancement for paraprofessionals is either severely limited or completely nonexistent because of the college-degree hurdle."[49]

It is to meet this problem that persons developing new careers programs have been turning. A recent survey of programs across the country found more than 20,000 employed paraprofessionals enrolled in degree-granting programs at more than 160 institutions of higher education.[50] As far as these programs relate to career advancement, 92 percent of the colleges reported that their programs were coordinated with employer career-ladder efforts.[51] However, only 57 percent of the colleges reported that promotions had occurred as a result of the college program.[52]

The apparent difference between the 92 percent of the programs which claim coordination of academic programs with the career-ladder and the only 57 percent which report promotions as a result of the academic program may be a function of several factors. First, given the newness of the [college] program—78 percent begun since 1968—there may not have been enough time for promotions. Second, the coordination may be more on paper than real as the fact 30 percent of the college program respondents could not reply to the question as to the effect upon promotions of the academic work indicates. Third, it may be, as the response of Alaska Methodist University stated, "agencies are slower to change than we are."[53]

Some of the more recent new careers programs, such as the Office of Education's Career Opportunities Program mentioned above, bring this connection between college and job much closer.

As impressive as are the reports of the paraprofessionals' effect on human service programs are their performances as college students. The Minneapolis program, where paraprofessionals attended the University of Minnesota's General College, reported:

> New Careerists, on the average, perform better than most junior college students and perform only slightly lower than University students taken as a group including freshmen, sophomores, juniors, and seniors.[54]

This finding of paraprofessionals doing as well as (or better than) traditional undergraduates is confirmed by the national study cited above. It reported that "60 percent of the paraprofessionals did as well, and 20 percent did better than students enrolled in similar courses."[55] Findings at Ohio State University reported that the dropout rate for paraprofessionals was substantially lower than for other students (11% and 40% respectively among freshmen).[56] This is also confirmed by the national study which reported that "at 50 percent of the schools, the paraprofessionals' rate was lower than for other students. It was the same at another 24 percent."[57]

In some college programs, paraprofessionals are bringing their expertise to bear as teachers. At the University of Minnesota's graduate program in urban studies, paraprofessionals (themselves undergraduates in the general college), are coteachers with traditional professors in several courses. They are paid as such, receive credit toward their own degree for the course, and have faculty club privileges. At Kent State, paraprofessionals in Akron act as field faculty to undergraduates in a community-studies course. And at New York University, paraprofessionals enrolled in a two-year Associate in Applied Sciences program act as consultants and advisers to a new liberal arts college undergraduate program in metropolitan studies.

In summarizing the performance of paraprofessionals as students, two leaders of the Minneapolis program wrote:

> the desire for education was the real sleeper of this particular program. Although the recruits were a relatively unselected group of marginally employed low-income adults who were not screened for any educational aptitude, the program tapped a deep vein of interest in higher education. These people were not unaware of the gate-keeping functions of education.[58]

Compared with the general college's average student, paraprofessionals scored higher on measures of motivation. They were also older and had an employment history; their fathers had lower occupational status; they were more likely to be Black and female; fewer had high school diplomas, and those who did ranked lower in their class; and they were more likely to be married.[59]

The rapid spread of college programs for paraprofessionals is illustrated in the mental health field where the first two-year program for mental health technicians began in 1966; there were 25 programs in 1969, and 57 in 1970.[60] In less than three years, the Head Start Supplementary Training Program involved nearly 300 institutions of higher education and more than 7,500 full-year Head Start employees.[61] In New Jersey, largely as a result of pressure from new careers program workers, a law was passed which allowed anyone over 19 years of age to attend a state community college regardless of whether they had a high school diploma or had passed the GED examination. And the Nassau County, New York, government now provides full tuition reimbursement and released-time arrangements to any county employee earning under $6,500. Perhaps most innovative is the establishment of a new careers college, the College of Human Services, which grew out of the new careers training work of the Women's Talent Corps.[62]

The effect of these college programs is not on the paraprofessional alone.

Despite many problems that the New Careers Program may present to the community college, it is evident that it is serving as a revitalizing influence. This infusion of new blood, new ideas, new teaching techniques, etc., has made Merritt College [California] more conscious of its function of a community college.[63]

Another author stated the following:

These disadvantaged students produce a stabilizing influence upon many of the radical youth on our campus. They challenge our instructors more than the average student and are more serious in their studies.[64]

With the development of additional college programs, the question of career ladders in agencies employing paraprofessionals as the sole route for their career advancement has become less critical. This is particularly true of the various new, nonresident programs. There is now Antioch College's University Without Walls, Goddard College's nonresident master's in Urban Education, nonresident undergraduate programs at the University of Oklahoma and the State College at Brockport, New York, and Syracuse University, as well as the newly funded (Carnegie and Ford Foundation) programs at the State University and State Education Department of New York.[65] The use of the College Level Equivalency Program is an important device for persons to gain college credit for knowledge acquired through means other than formal courses, as are the proposals for external-degree programs.

An even more basic question than what particular training or career route should be taken by paraprofessionals relates to the very quality of indigeneity which, we have seen, appears to be a central factor in their success as human service workers. It may be suggested that training and education may lead to a loss of the unique and desirable qualities of indigeneity. This view, however, assumes that the purpose and effect of the training is to "train out" the paraprofessionals' indigenous qualities. Of course, training can be designed to train in, to reinforce, to support such qualities. The education programs can and have been changed. And the training can incorporate the principles of cross-socialization where the indigenous worker learns from and teaches the professional, and vice versa. A separate question has to do with the resistance among some professionals to the upgrading of paraprofessionals. While unique and at a paraprofessional level, they may be seen as less of a threat to the professional.

COSTS AND BENEFITS

Estimating dollar value of human service programs is, in some ways, little more than an exercise in more or less educated guessing. However, if done carefully and accepted with due caution, it can give some indication of the parameters of the issue. And if, as we shall see is the case with cost-benefit analyses of paraprofessional programs, various studies done by different persons concerned with different population groups come up with reports in the same general range, we may temper somewhat our skeptical evaluation of such reports.

The Poverty Subcommittee of the Senate's Education and Labor Committee, in its report accompanying the Manpower Act of 1970, reported:

> We have estimated the present value of the direct social benefits from a public service job development program to be between $29,600 and $36,000 per new worker employed, and the costs of training him to be $3,000 to $7,000. . . . *A dollar invested now in a new worker from the urban ghetto may return anywhere from $4.23 to as much as $12.10 in extra gross national product.* [Emphasis in the original.][66]

A study of the new careers program in Minneapolis reports a return of from $1.04 to $1.59 per dollar invested.[67] The costs were estimated at $5,400 per trainee, which is more than $1,000 above the national average. On the estimated return side, the Minneapolis project had a lower percentage of welfare clients than the national average. Thus, the study author's avowal of a conservative estimate is correct: "An attempt was made to keep estimates of success rates and expected income at a conservative level." He goes on:

> It should be kept in mind that the project will undoubtedly yield a great many real benefits which cannot be readily quantified (such as influence on the trainees' own family and friends, probable decrease in need for law enforcement and other public services, etc.). [And he concludes:] A strong case can be made for considering the New Careers program a sound economic investment.[68]

The Project Crossroads program (Chapter 6) measured three types of program benefits: reduced costs due to diversion of cases from the criminal justice system; increased earnings or productivity due to job development and placement programs and higher employment rates over time due to lower recidivism; and reduced criminal justice system costs due to reduction in recidivism.[69] These three factors were incorporated in a benefit-to-cost index ratio which showed a ratio of from 2.2 to 1.8 depending on the rate of discount of future benefits.[70] Thus, even at the highest discount rate (15%), the program showed a significantly favorable benefit-to-cost ratio.

Another way of looking at benefits is presented in a report on MFY's Social Health Technician program.[71] The program started with 60 trainees; 41 (68 percent) completed the twenty-week training program. At the time of entry into the program, of these 41 persons, 35 were unemployed (16 on welfare) and the 6 who were employed earned a *total* annual income of less than $20,000. Twelve months after initial placement, 34 were holding training-related jobs and had an aggregate annual salary of $160,000. A year later, 36 were holding training-related jobs, and their annual aggregate earnings were $240,000.[72] Thus, from a total earned income of $20,000, the group of 41 went to an annual aggregate that represented a twelvefold increase—in less than three years.

Two California reports looked at individual aspects of the costs and benefits of paraprofessional programs. In describing the RODEO juvenile delinquency project (see Chapter 6), the Los Angeles County Personnel Director stated:

> In rough figures, each juvenile participant in this project represented a dollar savings of $1,300 per year to the county in services provided by the staff when compared to the costs of his residence in a camp. This was in spite of the fact that the reduction of caseload ratios and attachment of New Careers staff is substantially a more expensive staffing pattern than the department's traditional supervision program.[73]

And because the RODEO program, with its central feature the use of indigenous paraprofessionals, was more successful in working with juveniles than either the camps program or traditional supervision patterns, the cost-benefit ratio, if calculated, would appear to favor this approach.

As part of the Alameda County welfare aide project (see Chapter 6), an effort was made to calculate the potential dollar gain of participants attending college:

> Aides given 20 percent work-release time should be able to obtain their AA Degree in three years, the BA in six. The cost of the 20 percent work-release education plan, including per capita cost to the college, work time by the agency and incidental education expenses would total about $1,390 a year for junior college and $1,605 for senior college. The financial expense then for providing an aide with a BA Degree would be about $9,200. If they began work-release education at age 27, they would obtain their BA by age 33. The present value of estimated lifetime earnings of a 34-year-old college

graduate is $250,000, a figure $114,000 greater than their $136,000 expected lifetime earnings with only a high school education.[74]

COMMUNITY IDENTITY OF THE PARAPROFESSIONAL

We have already noted criticisms by Sherman Barr and Daniel and Laurel Tanner, who question the capability of those who have lived in the ghetto to perform effective human service work. We have also discussed Grosser's points which concern both quality of performance and the inflated view taken by the new careers movement. More specific are the problems noted in an evaluation of fifty-three New Careers programs which included the low percentage of male participants, low entry salaries, lack of changes in civil service practices, the limited nature of training, the lack of permanent positions after the federal subsidy period, and the limits of the ladders established.[75] The final report of the Minneapolis New Careers program offers some specific information on these and related points. Reporting on those who completed the two-year program, they stated:

> Enrollees finished about half the credits for a bachelor's degree on the average; they are generally in the fields of human service; and about half are still in school even though the program has ended. There was a substantial improvement in the average wages the enrollees earned, as well as a more steady form of employment for work.[76]

At their enrollment, over 50 percent of the participants were not self-supporting, and those who worked did so at an average salary of $1.98 per hour. At the end of the program, all but 14 percent were working, at an average salary of $3.14 per hour. Not only were more employed and at higher wages, but the positions were permanent, the jobs had more built-in advancement possibilities, and some worked at agencies which permitted released time for further education.[77]

More basic are the questions raised by Paul A. Kurzman. He cited reports by Grosser, Perry Levinson and Jeffery Schiller, and Pauline Coggs and Vivian R. Robinson, as to the tendency of paraprofessionals to identify with agency professionals. Kurzman then warned of the danger that in new careers programs (and social work efforts in general), social service efforts would overpower a social action emphasis.[78] As his purview seems to have been limited to social work, Kurzman appears not to have been familiar with the exhaustive Minneapolis data which showed an increasing community orientation of participants in new careers programs (see above), nor with such findings as those of Frederick L. Ahern, that, among paraprofessionals working in two New England community action programs, those who had been employed longest were highest in social activism.[79]

More important, however, than the adequacy of Kurzman's data as to what in fact happened to paraprofessionals when they worked in human service agencies, is the question of how to minimize deleterious effects on these workers, their commitment to social change, and to their communities. Surely one wants more than Kurzman's own suggestion that "social workers should commit their professional skill to organizing these indigenous workers."[80] More to the point is the organizing of paraprofessionals for their own ends under their own leadership and direction. This connection to the community is vividly expressed by a group of paraprofessionals employed by a community mental health center in New Haven, Connecticut.

> As a group, we were able to surmount many obstacles. Because of our ability to deal with professionals on a professional level, we decided to discard the stigma of being called "paraprofessionals." We do not feel, as that title insinuates, that we are less than fully qualified. We decided, to call ourselves "New Professionals."* With this new title, we became even more functional in order to live up to our new name and its connotations.
>
> To avoid falling into the same bag that other community professionals have, we must be constantly aware of our ultimate goal: to get the Black community on its feet economically and medically. The only way that we can do this is not to allow ourselves to be sucked into the Establishment. We must not allow the Establishment to use us to pacify the community. We must always work for the common good of our people, not becoming flunkies doing the dirty work of our agency to "cool out" the poor, especially Blacks. We must continually intervene in systems that are not truly concerned about the welfare of our people.[81]

A LOOK FORWARD

In 1960, paraprofessional programs were primarily concerned with the ability of traditional manpower to reach and serve new population groups, particularly the Blacks and the poor. This was contextualized and heightened by a sense of a professional manpower shortage. During the early part of the decade, concern for employment of the poor was added. This in turn produced the new careers effort with its tripartite focus to meet the individual's problem of poverty, the agency's manpower shortages, and the community's service needs. By 1970, while the three factors were still present, it were as if the kaleidoscope had turned a bit and the components were in different focus. No longer was it a matter of merely relieving the professional of the lower order of his work, nor was it a matter simply of using indigenous workers to herd their peers in for professionally manned services, nor was it a matter of individual escape from poverty.

---

*This title has also been adopted by the citywide organization of paraprofessionals in Pittsburgh, and the new paraprofessional section of the American Public Health Association, The New Professional Health Workers.

Increasingly, there was concern for the public work which needed to be done. A long list of national study commissions and presidential advisory bodies have identified the unfinished work. The most precise catalogue was produced by Harold Sheppard who conducted a survey of 130 cities. He asked chief executive officers the number of positions that could then be filled by nonprofessional workers to meet current needs.[82] The figures in Table 10 are low estimates in terms of total need, in that they are limited to municipal employment with present funds for programs existing in 1968 in 130 cities. One can estimate that the total figure would be increased manyfold if we were to include all other cities; county, state, and federal governments; and program areas expanded since 1968 such as pollution control, and use of paraprofessionals in health, education, and police work.

TABLE 10

Nonprofessional Public Service Job Possibilities, 1968

Category	Number
Antipollution enforcement	900
Education	39,134
Fire	5,390
General administration	5,313
Health and hospitals	18,790
Highway and/or traffic	7,179
Housing codes and inspection	1,473
Library	3,159
Police	11,161
Recreation and parks	14,359
Sanitation	7,534
Urban renewal	7,800
Welfare	18,497
Total	140,689

Note: Data based on 130 cities with populations of 100,000 or more.

Source: Harold L. Sheppard, *The Nature of the Job Problem and the Role of Public Service Employment* (Kalamazoo, Mich.: W. E. Upjohn Institute, 1969), p. 24.

Something of the range of new areas can be seen in the following job titles of positions held by paraprofessionals over period 1968-70: resident planner, legal service assistant, water pollution control operator, education administrator, community census enumerator, media technician, social health technician, urban technician, patient advocate, genetic assistant, and community advocate.[83]

While our concern has focused on public-sector work, the concepts can well be applied to the private sector. A comprehensive study of upgrading efforts in the private sector was conducted by E. F. Shelly and Company. They found that the main push for special training efforts had thus far come from "skill shortages and pressure from equal-employment-opportunity agencies." However, they also stated:

> [There are] clear indications of general worker discontent—productivity problems, absenteeism, turnover, behavioral problems, ever-increasing inflationary wage demands, a younger and brighter worker who is spurning job and institutional loyalties of previous generations.[84]

All of these are cited as reasons for giving increased attention to career-mobility efforts. A new careers program has been developed on a demonstration basis at Oxford Chemicals, Incorporated, a New Jersey firm which manufactures and prints plastics on complex, highspeed equipment.

> New employees have moved rapidly from enriched entry training into advanced skill training as a printer in 23 weeks compared to the traditional 3 or more years.
>
> The turnover rate for trainees was 20 percent lower as compared with the previous year.
>
> Subsequent employment history for those who left Oxford after completing training was significantly better in that they returned to school or found jobs while those that did not complete training experienced unemployment.
>
> In comparing the previous year's production with the period covered by the training program, production has increased 4.1 percent—this translates into an increased profit of $37,858 for Oxford.[85]

The program not only brings in new workers but can in various ways change the composition of the work force. Faced with a situation in the New York City public schools where, with a student population nearly 60 percent Black and Puerto Rican, only 9 percent of the teachers come from these groups, the City Commission on Human Rights was encouraging the rapid upgrading of the more than 15,000 paraprofessionals (most of whom were Black or Puerto Rican) as a way to integrate the school system's teaching staff.

Not only are the schools as employers being affected by paraprofessional programs but also, at their very heart, educational institutions are being affected. An early effort of the Howard University Institute for Youth Studies developed a new design for work-study programs in training for human-service work for seniors at the Cardozo High School, Washington, D.C.[86] And since 1969, increasing attention has been given to college programs for adults which either build on their previous work experience or combine study with their present work. The experience of the career-development facets of paraprofessional programs would seem to offer important guidelines for these new programs and they, in turn, surely will affect paraprofessional programs. While the exact nature of either of these prospects is not clear, it does seem apparent that the lock-step of work following schooling without the opportunity to combine the two or to move back and forth between the two is being broken.[8 7]

CONCLUSION

Whatever the broader effect of paraprofessional programs, however, we must come back to their work—how what they do affects the consumer of health, education, and welfare services. The preceding chapters surveyed a broad variety of material. A brief look at some of the more important studies may assist us in coming to at least tentative conclusions. In education, the careful examination of the Minneapolis kindergarten program, studies of paraprofessionals in elementary grades in Kentucky and Indiana, parents who received training and then helped their preschool youngsters in Florida, and the general examination of personnel in Adult Basic Education programs each gave evidence as to the effect of paraprofessional employment on pupil learning.

In mental health, the detailed study of one hospital by Robert B. Ellsworth described the effect of the old paraprofessionals; the work of Charles B. Truax described the value of the new paraprofessionals; and a national survey by Francine Sobey showed the broad effect of paraprofessionals in NIMH-funded programs. In addition, we noted individual efforts of indigenous paraprofessionals in community mental health at such programs as the Lincoln Hospital Mental Health Services, the Temple University Community Mental Health Center, and Harlem Hospital's Group Therapy Program.

In social work, the pioneering efforts of Mobilization for Youth, the nationwide Project Enable, and the detailed study of the Alameda County Welfare Department all offered impressive data.

In health programs, we saw a range of efforts that included upgrading nurses' aides to new positions, moving nurses and others to new roles as pediatric nurse assistants and physician's assistants, and new roles for indigenous workers in both community services and direct care. The Denver Comprehensive Health Center, New York City's Martin Luther King, Jr., Health Center, family planning outreach, the Contra Costa immunization program, and the Los Angeles anemia program provided reports of significant paraprofessional contributions.

The Manhattan Court Employment Project, Project Crossroads in Washington, D.C., J. Douglas Grant's pioneering program in the California Men's Prison, and the Los Angeles RODEO program provided data in the field of corrections.

A Wyoming vocational rehabilitation project suggests the broad range of service effected by paraprofessional efforts. Among those reported are that paraprofessionals contributed the following:

1. A useful adjunct to professional counselors rendering a higher quantitative and qualitative level of service to the disabled

2. Directly influential in providing vocational rehabilitation to a broader range of disabilities than had been the case prior to their use

3. Allowed counselors more time and effort with more seriously diabled clients

4. Themselves able to assist significantly more clients than had previously been the case.[8 8]

A part of this power must inevitably come from the efforts of the paraprofessionals themselves. A summary of a survey of early community action agency utilization of paraprofessionals stated:

Many of the nonprofessionals interviewed in this study have previously received other services aimed at reducing poverty. Some of them have been on welfare; others have lived in public housing projects, etc. Analysis of the interviews reveals that their response to their jobs as nonprofessionals appears to differ in fundamental ways from their response to receiving these other services. The other services ameliorated some of the worst effects of poverty, but did not mobilize the individual's own resources and capabilities for breaking out of the poverty cycle on their own initiative.[8 9]

We believe it is this tapping of deeper forces, in the end, that makes paraprofessional programs stand out. Human service practice is now being challenged from the community of users, especially the poor and minority groups, and in terms of the very values of professional practice. Unlike the forces for community control which come at the issues only from outside the service delivery systems, the paraprofessional effort comes at these problems with dimensions both from inside and outside the system. It brings to this challenge the power of both the community and the new workers.

In different ways, the introduction and utilization of indigenous paraprofessionals in each human service field, has been accompanied by a consideration of key questions on human service practice: How are present and potential users to be reached? What is to be offered and/or provided to them? Who is to do it? How and by whom are they to be trained? How is the delivery system to be organized, governed, and related to other systems? And, finally, how is the work done to be measured and evaluated? More than that, the introduction and implementation of paraprofessional programs, to borrow concepts from the physical sciences, would appear to have a catalytic, precipitant, and even synergetic effect. As he cuts across the various human-service fields and as he has a positive effect on the consumer—be it student, patient, or client—the paraprofessional is both a contributor and challenger at the very center of contemporary practice.

NOTES

1. Charles G. Grosser, *The Role of the Nonprofessional in the Manpower Development Programs* (Washington, D.C.: U.S. Department of Labor, 1966), pp. 49-50.

2. Robert Blauner and Anatole Shaffer, "New Careers and the Person" (Walnut Creek, Cal.: Contra Costa Council of Community Services, 1967), p. 40.

3. "Social-Psychological Changes in New Careerists" (Minneapolis: New Careers Research, University of Minnesota, 1969), p. 11.

4. Patricia Larson, "Discussions with New Careerists" (Minneapolis: New Careers Research, University of Minnesota, 1969), p. 6.

5. Gertrude S. Goldberg, "New Nonprofessionals in the Human Services: An Overview" (Washington, D.C.: Conference on the Use of Nonprofessionals in Mental Health Work: Consequences for Social Work and Psychology, American Psychological Association and National Association of Social Workers, 1967), p. 17.

6. Patricia Larson, Mary Bible, and R. Frank Falk, "Down the Up Staircase: A Study of New Careers Dropouts" (Minneapolis: New Careers Research, University of Minnesota, 1969), p. 5.

7. Margaret A. Thompson, "Contamination of New Careerists by Professionalization: Fact or Fancy?" (Minneapolis: New Careers Research, University of Minnesota, 1969), p. 56.

8. Arthur Pearl and Frank Riessman, *New Careers for the Poor: The Nonprofessional in Human Service* (New York: Free Press, 1965), p. 197.

9 Thompson, *op. cit.,* p. 2.

10. *Ibid.,* pp. 38, 56.

11. *Ibid.,* pp. 60-61.

12. *Ibid.,* p. 64.

13. *Ibid.,* p. 68.

14. *Ibid.,* pp. 68-70.

15. *Ibid.,* p. 70.

16. *Ibid.*, p. 72.

17. *Ibid.*, p. 74.

18. *Ibid.*, p. 5.

19. "Report of the Institute for Community Studies, Queens College," cited in *New Human Services Newsletter,* I, 1 (Fall, 1970).

20. Grosser, *op. cit.,* p. 48.

21. Charles G. Grosser, "Manpower Development Programs," in Charles G. Grosser *et al.,* eds., *Nonprofessionals in the Human Services* (San Francisco: Jossey-Bass, Inc., 1969), pp. 128-29.

22. *Ibid.,* p. 129.

23. *Ibid.,* p. 130.

24. Grosser, *Role of the Nonprofessional, op. cit.,* p. 50.

25. "Office of New Careers," *New Careers Newsletter,* III, 6 (Fall, 1969), 2.

26. *New Careers and HEW* (Washington, D.C.: U.S. Department of Health, Education, and Welfare, 1970), p. iii.

27. "California Boosts New Careers," *New Careers Newsletter,* II, 2 (Summer, 1968), 2.

28. "Testimony on Public Service Work," *New Careers Newsletter,* IV, 2 (Spring, 1970), 4.

29. *Public Service Jobs for Urban Ghetto Residents* (Washington, D.C.: National Civil Service League, 1969); see also, the issues of its journal, *Good Government.*

30. See "Civil Service Strategy: Ten Rules," *New Human Services Newsletter,* I, 2 (Winter, 1979), 5.

31. The publications of the National Civil Service League report on these developments, as does the *New Human Services Newsletter.*

32. Ohio Education Association, *Educational Aides,* Research Bulletin No. 5 (Columbus, 1970).

33. National Institute for New Careers, *New Careers in Social Welfare: A Status Report* (Washington, D.C.: University Research Corporation, 1970), p. 5.

34. *Ibid.,* p. 6.

35. Council on Social Work Education, *Guidelines for Associate Degree Programs in Community and Social Services* (New York, 1970).

36. *New Careers Newsletter,* IV, 2 (Spring, 1970), p. 6.

37. "Paraprofessionals and Professional Organizations: 'Back of the Bus' or 'First Class' ", *New Human Services Newsletter,* I, 2 (Winter, 1970), 7.

38. *Ibid.*

39. *Ibid.*

40. Cited in "AMA Guidelines," *New Careers Newsletter,* IV, 2 (Spring, 1970), 3; see also, National Institute for New Careers, *New Careers in Health: A Status Report* (Washington, D.C.: University Research Corporation, 1970), p. 26.

41. John H. Starie and Margaret Stevenson, "Local Associations Ask About Paraprofessionals," *National Education Association Journal,* LVI, 6 (September, 1967), 74; see also, "Paraprofessionals and Professional Organizations," *loc. cit.*

42. "Paraprofessionals' Unions Win Big Wage Increases," *New Careers Newsletter,* IV, 4 (Special Issue), 1.

43. Joan Grant, *A Strategy for California's Use of Training Resources in the Development of New Careers for the Poor* (Sacramento: Institute for the Study of Crime and Delinquency, New Careers Development Project, 1966), p. 16.

44. National Institute for New Careers, *An Assessment of Technical Assistance and Training Needs in New Careers Projects Being Sponsored by the United States Training and Employment Service, Manpower Administration, U.S. Department of Labor* (Washington, D.C.: University Research Corporation, 1969), p. 3.

45. New Careers Development Center, *New Careers, 1968-69, A Report to the Ford Foundation* (New York: New York University, 1969), p. 10.

46. National Committee on Employment for Youth, *Career Mobility for Paraprofessionals in Human Service Agencies* (Washington, D.C.: U.S. Department of Labor, 1969).

47. *Ibid.,* p. 55.

48. *Ibid.,* Table C.

49. *New York Times,* March 1, 1970.

50. Alan Gartner and Harriet Johnston, *An Examination of College Programs for Paraprofessionals* (New York: New Careers Development Center, New York University, 1970).

51. *Ibid.,* Table 12.

52. *Ibid.,* Table 13.

53. *Ibid.,* p. 15.

54. Edward Knop *et al.,* "New Careerists in Higher Education" (Minneapolis: New Careers Research, University of Minnesota, 1969), p. 3.

55. Gartner and Johnson, *op. cit.,* p. i.

56. Sheldon S. Steinberg, "Stresses, Strains, and Joys of Utilizing Auxiliary Personnel," *Journal of Home Economics,* LXII, 2 (February, 1970), 100.

57. Gartner and Johnson, *loc. cit.*

58. William S. Bennett, Jr. and R. Frank Falk, *New Careers and Urban Schools* (New York: Holt, Rinehart, and Winston, 1970), p. 168.

59. Knop *et al., op. cit.,* pp. 14-16.

60. National Institute for New Careers, *New Careers in Mental Health, A Status Report* (Washington, D.C.: University Research Corporation, 1970), p. 16.

61. John C. Flynn, "Head Start Supplementary Training: From Aloofness to Commitment," *Head Start Career Developments,* I, 5 (April, 1970), 3.

62. Joseph Featherstone, "The Talent Corps: Career Ladder for Bottom Dogs," *New Republic,* CLXI, 10 (September 13, 1969), 17-23.

63. Don Richardson, "New Careers: An Instrument for Change in the Community College," in *Some Who Dared: Community College Programs for Public Service Occupations* (Berkeley, Cal.: Institute for Local Self-Government, 1970), p. 91.

64. Nowell Smith, "Public Employment and the Disadvantaged: Taking the Risk," in *Public Service Employment and the Disadvantaged* (Berkeley, Cal.: Institute for Local Self-Government, 1970), pp. 4-5.

65. See "Get the Degree, Skip the Ladder," *New Human Services Newsletter,* I, 1 (Fall, 1970), 4; see also, *New York Times,* February 23, 1971.

66. Cited in *New Human Services Newsletter*, I, 1 (Fall, 1970), 2. Projected figures seem to be derived from the following National Civil Service League Study of ongoing paraprofessional programs: Bennett Harrison, "Public Employment and the Disadvantaged—Public Service Jobs for Urban Ghetto Residents," *Good Government*, LXXXVI, 3 (Fall, 1969), 17-18.

67. Ronald S. Brandt, "Costs and Benefits of the Minneapolis New Careers Program" (Minneapolis: New Careers Research, University of Minnesota, 1968, mimeographed), p. 5.

68. *Ibid.*, p. 6.

69. John F. Holahan, *A Benefit-Cost Analysis of Project Crossroads* (Washington, D.C.: National Committee for Children and Youth, 1970), *passim.*

70. *Ibid.*, p. 63.

71. Anita Vogel, *Establishing a New Career: The Social Health Technician* (New York: Mobilization for Youth, 1970).

72. *Ibid.*, pp. 3-4.

73. Gordon Nestig, "Testimony Presented Before the U.S. Senate Labor Committee, Sub-Committee on Manpower," Los Angeles, January 7, 1970.

74. Dorthea Cudaback, "Work-Release Education for Welfare Aides: A Sound Investment" (Richmond: School of Social Work, University of California, 1969).

75. National Institute for New Careers, *An Assessment, op. cit.*, p. 8.

76. Margaret A. Thompson, "The Minneapolis New Careers Program: A Follow-Up Study" (Minneapolis: Office of Career Development, University of Minneapolis, 1971), p. 13.

77. *Ibid.*, pp. 5-7.

78. Paul A. Kurzman, "The New Careers Movement and Social Change," *Social Casework*, LI, 1 (January, 1970), pp. 22-27; Charles G. Grosser, "Local Residents as Mediators Between Middle-Class Professional Workers and Lower-Class Clients," *Social Service Review*, XL, 1 (March, 1966), 62; Perry Levinson and Jeffery Schiller, "Role Analysis of the Indigenous Nonprofessional," *Social Work*, XI, 3 (July, 1966), 99; and Pauline Coggs and Vivian R. Robinson, "Training Indigenous Community Leaders for Employment in Social Work," *Social Casework*, XLVIII, 5 (May, 1967), 281.

79. Frederick L. Ahearn, Jr., "Paraprofessionals: Anomie and Activism," paper presented at the National Conference of Social Welfare, Chicago, June 1, 1970, p. 10.

80. Kurzman, *op. cit.*, p. 27.

81. Roberta Boyette *et al.*, "The Plight of the New Careerist," *American Journal of Orthopsychiatry*, XLI, 2 (March, 1971), 237-38.

82. Harold L. Sheppard, *The Nature of the Job Problem and the Role of Public Service Employment* (Kalamazoo, Mich.: W. E. Upjohn Institute, 1969), p. 24.

83. *New Careers Newsletter, passim.*

84. Cited in the *New York Times,* March 7, 1971, Section I, Part 2, p. 63.

85. "New Careers in Industry," *New Human Services Newsletter,* I, 1 (Fall, 1970), Special Insert; see also, Lee Jacobson, "New Careers," *Training in Business and Industry,* VII, 8 (August, 1970), 24-33.

86. William H. Denham *et al.*, "High School Training for New Careers in Human Services," *The National Elementary Principal,* XLVI, 6 (May, 1967), 22-28.

87. Alan Gartner, "New Patterns for Young and Old," *New Generation,* XLXI, 1 (Winter, 1969).

88. "Providing Vocational Rehabilitation Services in Sparsely Settled Areas of Wyoming" (Cheyenne: Final Report, The Wyoming Aide Project, Division of Vocational Rehabilitation, State Department of Education, 1969), especially pp. 60-61.

89. Daniel Yankelovich, Inc., *A Study of Nonprofessionals in the CAP* (New York, 1966), pp. 106-7.

BIBLIOGRAPHY

Abbott, Margaret. *The Teacher and His Staff*. Grand Forks, N.D.: Grand Forks Public Schools, 1969.

Adelson, Gerald, and Anthony R. Kovner. "The Social Health Technician: A New Occupation," *Social Casework*, L, 7 (July, 1969), 395-400.

Ahearn, Frederick L., Jr. "Paraprofessionals: Anomie and Activism." Paper presented at the National Conference of Social Welfare, Chicago, June 1, 1970.

Aides to Teachers and Children. Washington, D.C.: Association for Childhood Education International, 1968.

Albee, George W. "The Miracle of the Loaves and the Fishes Updated: Nonprofessionals for Everyone!" *American Journal of Orthopsychiatry*, XXXIX, 2 (March, 1969), 331-32.

Alexander, S. Kern. "What Teacher Aides Can—And Cannot Do," *Nation's Schools*, LXXXII, 2 (April, 1968), 23-26.

"Allied Health Workers in Pediatric Practice." Chicago: American Academy of Pediatrics, 1969.

American Institute for Research. "A Study of Selected Programs for the Education of Disadvantaged Children." Palo Alto, Cal., 1968.

An Annotated Bibliography on Auxiliary Personnel in Education. New York: Bank Street College of Education, 1969.

An Annotated Bibliography: Public Employment and the Disadvantaged. Washington, D.C.: National Civil Service League, 1970.

Anastasiou, Nicholas J. *An Evaluation of the Kindergarten Teacher Assistant Project*. Palo Alto, Cal.: Palo Alto Unified School District, 1966.

Anderson, Robert. "Organizational Characteristics of Education—Staff, Utilization and Development," *Review of Educational Research*, XXXIV, 4 (October, 1964), 455-69.

Androvic, Michael P., and Bernard Guerney, Jr. "A Psychotherapeutic Aide in a Head Start Program, Part I, Theory and Practice," *Children*, XVI, 1 (January-February, 1969), 14-17.

Arcement, Sr. Genevieve. "A Teacher Aide Program That Really Works," *Catholic School Journal*, LX, 10 (December, 1969), 26-27.

Aronowitz, Stanley. "Mobilization for Youth's New Model for Subprofessional Training: Its Impact on New York City's Health Services." New York: Mobilization for Youth, 1968. Mimeographed.

Arth, Alfred A., *et al. Teacher Aides: The Preparation and Utilization of Paraprofessionals*. Charlottesville: Curry Memorial School of Education, University of Virginia, 1970.

Auxiliary Personnel in Education: Their Present and Potential Contributions in the Philadelphia Schools. Philadelphia: The School District of Philadelphia, 1968.

"Auxiliary School Personnel," *The National Elementary Principal*, XLVI, 6 (May, 1967), 6-12.

Auxiliary School Personnel, A Statement by the National Commission on Teacher Education and Professional Standards. Washington, D.C.: National Education Association, 1967.

Ballard, Kelley B., and Sam R. Alley. "Pilot Evaluation of Selected New Careers Projects." Washington, D.C.: AVCO Economic Systems Corporation, 1968.

Barker, Robert L., and Thomas L. Briggs. *Differential Use of Social Work Manpower*. New York: National Association of Social Workers, 1968.

Barney, Helen S. "The Use of Nutrition and Home Economics Aides in Maternity and Infant Care and Children and Youth Projects," *Journal of Home Economics*, LXII, 2 (February, 1970), 114-19.

Barr, Sherman. "A Professional Takes a Second Look," *American Child*, XLIX, 1 (Winter, 1967), 14-17.

———. *Some Observations on the Practice of Nonprofessional Workers*. New York: Mobilzation for Youth, 1966.

Battle, Mark. "The Pitfalls," *American Child*, XLIX, 1 (Winter, 1967), 17-19.

Bauman, Gerald, and Vera Douthit. "Use of a Non-Medical Community Setting to Differentiate and Develop Patient and Client Roles in the Rehabilitation of Psychiatric Patients." Paper presented at the Annual Meeting, American Orthopsychiatric Association, March, 1968.

Bayer, Alan E., and Lyle F. Schoenfeldt. "Student Interchangeability in Three-Year and Four-Year Nursing Programs," *The Journal of Human Resources*, V, 1 (Winter, 1970), 71-88.

Beavers, Irene. "An Overview," *Journal of Home Economics*, LXII, 2 (February, 1970), 83-84.

Beck, Bertram M., *et al. New Health Occupations Program: Report to the Office of Economic Opportunity and Proposal for a One Year Demonstration*. New York: Mobilization for Youth, 1968.

Bellin, Lowell Eliezer. "The New Left and American Public Health—Attempted Radicalization of the APHA Through Dialectic," *American Journal of Public Health*, LX, 6 (June, 1970), 973-81.

————, *et al.* "Preparing Public Health Subprofessionals Recruited for the Poverty Group—Lessons from an OEO Work-Study Program," *American Journal of Public Health*, LVII, 2 (February, 1967), 242-52.

Benjamin, Judith G., *et al. Pros and Cons: New Roles for Nonprofessionals in Corrections*. Washington, D.C.: Office of Juvenile Delinquency and Youth Development, U.S. Department of Health, Education, and Welfare, 1966.

Bennett, William S., Jr., and R. Frank Falk. *New Careers and Urban Schools*. New York: Holt, Rinehart, and Winston, 1970.

Bhaerman, Robert D. *Several Educators' Cure for the Common Cold, Among Other Things One Unionist's View of Staff Differentiation*. "Quest Papers," No. 7. Washington, D.C.: American Federation of Teachers, n.d.

————. *A Study Outline on Differentiated Staffing*. "Quest Report," No. 2. Washington, D.C.: American Federation of Teachers, n.d.

Birnbaum, Martin L., and Chester H. Jones. "Activities of the Social Work Aide," *Social Casework*, XLVIII, 10 (December, 1967), 626-32.

Blessing, Kenneth R. "Use of Teacher Aides in Special Education: A Review and Possible Applications," *Exceptional Children*, XXXIV, 2 (October, 1967), 107-13.

Blum, Arthur. "Differentiated Use of Manpower in Public Welfare," *Social Work*, XI, 1 (January, 1966), 16-21.

Blum, Henrik L., *et al.* "The Multi-Purpose Worker and the Neighborhood Multi-Service Center: Initial Experiences and Implications of the RODEO Community Service Center," *American Journal of Public Health*, LVIII, 3 (March, 1968), 458-68.

Borstal, Rodney M., and John A. Dewar. "The Paraprofessional and the States," *The National Elementary Principal*, XLIX, 5 (April, 1970), 63-67.

Bouhoutsos, Jacqueline C. "The Non-Traditionally Trained Mental Health Worker: Fad or Future?" *American Journal of Orthopsychiatry*, XL, 2 (March, 1970), 297-98.

Bowman, Garda W., and Gordon J. Klopf. *Auxiliary School Personnel: Their Roles, Training, and Institutionalization*. New York: Bank Street College of Education, 1967.

————. *New Careers and Roles in the American School: A Study of Auxiliary Personnel in Education*. New York: Bank Street College of Education, 1968.

Boyette, Roberta. "The Plight of the New Careerist," *American Journal of Orthopsychiatry*, XLI, 2 (March, 1971), 237-38.

Brager, George. "The Indigenous Worker: A New Approach for the Social Work Technician," *Social Work*, X, 2 (April, 1965), 33-40.

————. "New Concepts and Patterns of Service: The Mobilization for Youth Program." *Mental Health of the Poor: New Treatment Approaches for Low Income People*. Edited by Frank Riessman, Jerome Cohen, and Arthur Pearl. New York: Free Press, 1964.

Brandt, Ronald S. "Costs and Benefits of The Minneapolis New Careers Program." Minneapolis: New Careers Research, University of Minnesota, 1968. Mimeographed.

Brazelton, Elizabeth W. "Teacher Aide Effects on Language Development in Head Start Children." Unpublished thesis, Auburn University, 1969.

Brenner, Marcella, *et al. Teacher Aides in Action in Elementary and Secondary Schools*. Washington, D.C.: Washington School of Psychiatry, 1969.

Brightman, I., *et al.* "Knowledge and Utilization of Health Resources by Public Assistance Recipients," *American Journal of Public Health and the Nation's Health*, LXXIII, 10 (October, 1968), 919-25.

Brion, Helen. "The New Professional Assistant in School Health Services," *Journal of School Health*, XXXVIII, 5 (May, 1968), 278-86.

Bureau of School and Cultural Research. *Survey of Public School Teacher Aides, Fall, 1965.* Albany: State Education Department, 1966.

California Teachers Association. *Salaries Paid Teachers Aides in California School Districts, 1967-68.* "Research Bulletin," No. 227. Burlingame: California Teachers Association, 1968.

————. *Teacher Aides in California Schools and School Districts, 1966-67.* "Research Bulletin," No. 206. Burlingame: California Teachers Association, 1967.

Callan, Laurence B. "Health Education Aide Trainee Project," *Public Health Reports*, LXXXIV, 5 (May, 1969), 459-64.

Canfield, James. "The High Cost of Non-Teaching Assignments," *The Clearing House*, XLIV, 5 (January, 1970), 296-99.

Carkhuff, Robert R. "Differential Functioning of Lay and Professional Helpers," *Journal of Counseling Psychology*, XV, 2 (March, 1968), 117-26.

————, and Andrew Griffin. "The Selection and Training of Human Relations Specialists," *Journal of Counseling Psychology*, XVII, 5 (September, 1970), 443-50.

Career Opportunities in Service to the Disadvantaged and Handicapped. Washington, D.C.: Office of Education, U.S. Department of Health, Education, and Welfare, 1969.

Center for the Study of Liberal Education for Adults. *Essays on New Careers: Social Implications for Adult Educators.* Syracuse: Syracuse University, 1970.

Chaplan, Abraham A., *et al.* "The Role of Volunteers in Community Mental Health Programs," *Community Mental Health Journal*, II, 3 (Fall, 1966), 255-58.

Christmas, June Jackson. "Group Methods in Teaching and Practice: Nonprofessional Mental Health Personnel in a Deprived Community," *American Journal of Orthopsychiatry*, XXXVI, 3 (April, 1966), 410-19.

"Classroom Helpers Prove Their Worth," *North Carolina Education*, XXX, 1 (September, 1966).

The Classroom Teacher Speaks on His Supportive Staff. Washington, D.C.: Department of Classroom Teachers, National Education Association, 1967.

Cloward, Richard A., and Lloyd E. Ohlin. *Opportunity and Delinquency: A Theory of Delinquent Gangs*. Glencoe, Ill.: The Free Press, 1960.

Coate, Shirley, and Eugene A. Nordstrom, Jr. "Experiment in Upgrading The Nonprofessional Worker," *Social Casework*, L, 7 (July, 1969), 401-6.

Coggs, Pauline, and Vivian R. Robinson. "Training Indigenous Community Leaders for Employment in Social Work," *Social Casework*, XLVIII, 5 (May, 1967), 278-81.

Cohen, Audrey C. "The College for Human Services," *The Record*, LXIX, 7 (April, 1968), 665-82.

Colorado Department of Education. *The Use of Teacher Aides in Colorado*. Denver, 1968.

Cooper, C. "The Chicago YMCA Detached Workers: Current Status of an Action Program." Paper presented to the American Sociological Association, Annual Meeting, Los Angeles, 1963.

"A Cooperative Study for the Better Utilization of Teacher Competencies." Mount Pleasant: Central Michigan University, 1960.

Council on Social Work Education, *Guidelines for Associate Degree Programs in Community and Social Services*. New York, 1970.

Cowen, Emory L., *et al.* "A College Student Volunteer Program in the Elementary School Setting," *Community Mental Health Journal*, II, 4 (Winter, 1966), 319-28.

Coye, Robert D., and Marc F. Hansen. "The 'Doctor's Assistant,' " *Journal of the American Medical Association*, CCIX, 4 (July 28, 1969), 529-33.

Craig, Sally K. *Bibliography for Use in Head Start Training and Career Development*. Washington, D.C.: University Research Corporation, 1970.

Cudaback, Dorthea. "Case-Sharing in the AFDC Program: The Use of Welfare Service Aides," *Social Work*, XIV, 3 (July, 1969), 93-99.

————. "Summary Report in Welfare Service Aide Project." Richmond: School of Social Welfare, University of California, 1968. Mimeographed.

————. "Training and Education of New Careerists in Public Welfare." Richmond: School of Social Work, University of California, 1969. Mimeographed.

————. "Work-Release Education for Welfare Aides: A Social Investment." Richmond: School of Social Work, University of California, 1969. Mimeographed.

Cutler, Marilyn H. "National Report Shows Teacher Aides Are Worth The Effort," *The Nation's Schools,* LXXIII, 4 (April, 1964), 67-69.

Dady, Milan B. *Auxiliary Personnel Programs in Rural America.* Morehead, Ky.: Morehead State University, 1968.

————. *Director's Report: Institute for Support Personnel.* Morehead, Ky.: Morehead State University, 1970.

Davidoff, Ida F. *et al.* "The Mental Health Rehabilitation Worker: A New Member of The Psychiatric Team," *Community Mental Health Journal,* V, 1 (January, 1969), 46-54.

Davis, Calvin E. "The Rehabilitation Aide in a Rural Poverty Area," *Rehabilitation Record,* IX, 2 (March-April, 1968), 36-37.

Davis, Donald A. "The Fennville Teacher Aide Experiment," *The Journal of Teacher Education,* XIII, 2 (June, 1962), 187-90.

Deason, John. "What They Say About Teacher Aides," *School Executive* (December, 1957), 68-70.

Decade of Experiment: The Fund for the Advancement of Education, 1951-61. New York: Ford Foundation, 1961.

del Valle, Allive, and Felton Alexander. "Effects of the Project on Family Service Agencies and Urban Leagues," *Social Casework,* XLVIII, 10 (December, 1967), 633-38.

Denemark, George W. "The Teacher and His Staff," *NEA Journal,* LV, 9 (December, 1966) 17-19.

Denham, William H., *et al.* "High School Training for New Careers in Human Services," *The National Elementary Principal,* XLVI, 6 (May, 1967), 22-28.

Dillingham, John C., and Sandra Sutherland. "Mental Health Skill Training for Nonprofessionals: A Response to Community Need, A Challenge to Professional Teaching Traditions," *American Journal of Orthopsychiatry,* XXXIX, 2 (March, 1969), 355-56.

Domke, Herbert R., and Gladys Coffey. "The Neighborhood-Based Public Health Worker: Additional Manpower for Community Health Services," *American Journal of Public Health,* LVI, 4 (April, 1966), 603-8.

The Education Professions, An Annual Report on the People Who Serve Our Schools and Colleges, 1969-70. Washington, D.C.: Office of Education, U.S. Department of Health, Education, and Welfare, 1970.

Eisdorfer, Carl, and Stuart E. Golann. "Principles for the Training of 'New Professionals' in Mental Health," *Community Mental Health Journal*, V, 5 (May, 1969), 349-57.

Ellsworth, Robert B. *Nonprofessionals in Psychiatric Rehabilitation*. New York: Appleton-Century-Crofts, 1968.

Elston, Patricia. "Public Welfare: The Breath of Change." *Up From Poverty: New Career Ladders for Nonprofessionals*. Edited by Frank Riessman and Hermine I. Popper. New York: Harper and Row, 1968.

Emerling, Frank C., and Kanawha Z. Chavis. "The Teacher Aide," *Educational Leadership*, XXIV, 2 (November, 1966), 175-83.

Engbreton, William E. "Creative Programs in Teacher Education," *NEA Journal*, LV, 9 (December, 1966), 45-47.

Engelkes, James R., and Ralph R. Roberts. "Rehabilitation Counselor's Level Training and Job Performance," *Journal of Counseling Psychology*, XVII, 6 (November, 1970), 522-26.

Epstein, Laura. "Differential Use of Staff: A Method to Expand Social Services," *Social Work*, VII, 4 (October, 1962), 66-72.

Erickson, E. *Summary Report: Teacher and Teacher Aides Studies*. Grand Rapids, Mich.: Grand Rapids Educational Studies Center, 1968.

Esbensen, Thornwald. "Should Teacher Aides Be More Than Clerks?" *Phi Delta Kappan*, XLVII, 5 (January, 1966), 237.

Estes, E. H., Jr., "Advantages and Limitations of Medical Assistants," *Journal of the American Geriatric Society*, XVI, 10 (October, 1968), 1083-87.

————. "The Duke Physician Assistant Program: A Progess Report," *Archives of Environmental Health*, XVII, 11 (November, 1968), 690-91.

Exemplary Education for Early Childhood. Greeley, Col.: Weld County School District, 1968.

Farmer, James. "Demand for Health Services Creates Medical Manpower Crisis." *Afro-American Newspaper*, September, 1969, p. 90.

Farrar, Marcella, and Mary L. Hemmy. "Use of Nonprofessional Staff in Work with the Aged," *Social Work*, VIII, 3 (July, 1963), 42-48.

Faust, Charles. "Utilization of Teaching Resources in Secondary Schools," *California Journal of Secondary Education*, XXXII, 5 (May, 1957), 292-94.

"The Feasibility of Training Non-Skilled Personnel to Assist Professional Staff in the Care and Treatment of Mentally Retarded Children." Final Report of a Child Welfare Demonstration Project. New York: Retarded Infants Service, Inc., 1967.

Featherstone, Joseph. "The Talent Corps: Career Ladder for Bottom Dogs," *New Republic*, CLXI, 10 (September 13, 1969), 17-23.

Fendall, N. R. E. "Auxiliary Health Personnel: Training and Use," *Public Health Reports*, LXXXII, 6 (June, 1967), 471-79.

Ferver, Jack, and Doris M. Cook. *Teacher Aides: Handbook for Instructors and Administrators*. Madison: Center for Extension Programs in Education, The University of Wisconsin, 1968.

"Field Test and Evaluation of Selected Adult Basic Education Systems." New York: Greenleigh Associates, Inc., 1966.

Fine, Sidney. "Guidelines for Designing New Careers," *Journal of Home Economics*, LXII, 2 (February, 1970), 103-7.

––––––. *Guidelines for the Design of New Careers*. Kalamazoo, Mich.: The W. E. Upjohn Institute for Employment Research, 1967.

Fisher, John K. "Subprofessionals in Pupil Personnel Services," *NASSP Bulletin*, LII, 324 (January, 1968), 49-57.

Fishman, Jacob R. and John McCormack. "Mental Health Without Walls: Community Mental Health in the Ghetto," *American Journal of Psychiatry*, CXXVI, 10 (April, 1970), 1461-67.

––––––, and Lonnie E. Mitchell. "New Careers for the Disadvantaged." Paper presented at the Annual Meeting of the American Psychiatric Association, San Francisco, Cal., May 13, 1970.

Flynn, John C. "Head Start Supplementary Training: From Aloofness to Commitment," *Head Start Career Developments*, I, 5 (April, 1970).

Furuno, Setsu, and Augie Connor. "Use of Nonprofessional Personnel for Health Screening of Head Start Children," *American Journal of Orthopsychiatry*, XL, 2 (March, 1970), 300-2.

Gales, Harriet. "The Community Health Education Project: 'Bridging The Gap'", *American Journal of Public Health*, LX, 2 (February, 1970), 322-27.

Gamon, Thomas M., S.J. "The Role of the Nonprofessional in the Harlem Domestic Peace Corps," *Sociology and Social Research*, LII, 4 (July, 1968), 349-62.

Garfield, Sidney, R. "The Delivery of Medical Care," *Scientific American*, CCXXII, 4 (April, 1970), 15-23.

Garfield, Sol L. "New Developments in the Preparation of Counselors," *Community Mental Health Journal*, V, 3 (June, 1969), 240-46.

Gartner, Alan. *Do Paraprofessionals Improve Human Services? A First Critical Appraisal of the Data*. New York: New Careers Development Center, New York University, 1969.

————. "New Patterns for Young and Old," *New Generation*, XLXI, 1 (Winter, 1969).

————, and Harriet Johnson. *An Examination of College Programs for Paraprofessionals*. New York: New Careers Development Center, New York University, 1970.

————, Mary Conway Kohler, and Frank Riessman, *Children Teach Children: Learning Through Teaching*. New York: Harper and Row, 1971.

Glovinsky, Arnold, and Joseph P. Johns. "Paraprofessionals: Twenty-six Ways to Use Them," *School Management*, XIII, 2 (February, 1966), 46-69.

Goldberg, Gertrude S. "New Nonprofessionals in the Human Services: An Overview." Conference on the Use of Nonprofessionals in Mental Health Work: Consequences for Social Work and Psychology. Washington, D.C.: American Psychological Association and National Association of Social Workers, 1967.

————. "Nonprofessionals in Human Services." *Nonprofessionals in the Human Services*. Edited by Charles G. Grosser *et al*. San Francisco: Jossey-Bass, Inc., 1969.

Goldstein, David H. "Teacher Aides," *The Instructor*, LXXVI, 2 (October, 1966), 31-32.

Gordon, Jesse E. "Project Cause, The Federal Anti-Poverty Program, and Some Implications of Subprofessional Training." *Psycho-Therapeutic Agents: New Roles for Nonprofessionals, Parents, and Teachers.* Edited by Bernard G. Guerney, Jr. New York: Holt, Rinehart, and Winston, 1969.

Gottesfeld, Harry, *et al*. "A Study of the Role of Paraprofessionals in Community Mental Health," *Community Mental Health Journal*, VI, 4 (August, 1970), 285-91.

Goulet, Richard R. "Cultivating A New Crop of Human Resources with ESEA Title III," *The National Elementary Principal*, XLVI, 6 (May, 1967), 49-52.

Grambs, Jean D. *Paraprofessionals and Teacher Aides: An Annotated Bibliography*. Washington, D.C.: ERIC Clearinghouse on Teacher Education, 1970.

Grant, J. Douglas. "The Offender as a Correctional Manpower Resource." *Up From Poverty: New Career Ladders for Nonprofessionals*. Edited by Frank Riessman and Hermine I. Popper. New York: Harper and Row, 1968.

Grant, Joan. *A Strategy for California's Use of Training Resources in the Development of New Careers for the Poor*. Sacramento: Institute for the Study of Crime and Delinquency, New Careers Development Project, 1966.

Greenberg, Barry. "Review of Literature Relating to the Use of Nonprofessionals in Education (From 1942 to 1967)." New York: New Careers Development Center, New York University, 1967.

Grisvold, James. "The Detroit DVR Responds to the Inner City Challenge," *Rehabilitation Record*, X, 3 (May-June, 1969), 33-37.

Grosser, Charles G. "Class Orientation of the Indigenous Staff." *Community Action Against Poverty*. Edited by George Brager and Francis P. Purcell. New Haven: College and University Press, 1967.

————. "Local Residents as Mediators Between Middle-Class Professional Workers and Lower-Class Clients," *Social Service Review*, XL, 1 (March, 1966), 56-63.

————. *The Role of the Nonprofessional in the Manpower Development Programs*. Washington, D.C.: U.S. Department of Labor, 1966.

————, *et al.*, eds. *Nonprofessionals in the Human Services*. San Francisco: Jossey-Bass, Inc., 1969.

Guerney, Bernard F., Jr., ed. *Psychotherapeutic Agents: New Roles for Nonprofessionals, Parents, and Teachers*. New York: Holt, Rinehart, and Winston, 1969.

Guidelines for Career Development of Auxiliary Personnel in Education. Albany, N.Y.: State Department of Education, 1968.

Hadley, John, *et al.* "An Experiment in the Education of the Preprofessional Mental Health Worker: The Purdue Program," *Community Mental Health Journal*, VI, 1 (February, 1970), 40-50.

Hallowitz, Emanuel. "The Expanding Role of the Neighborhood Service Center." *Up From Poverty: New Career Ladders for Nonprofessionals*.

Frank Riessman and Hermine I. Popper. New York: Harper and Row, 1968.

———. "The Neighborhood Service Center: A New Community Mental Health Approach." New York, Unpublished MS, n.d.

———, and Frank Riessman. "The Role of the Indigenous Nonprofessional in a Community Mental Health Center Program." Paper presented to the American Orthopsychiatric Association Annual Meeting, San Francisco, 1966.

———, et al. "Neighborhood Service Center Program." New York: Lincoln Hospital Mental Health Services, 1965.

Halpern, Werner I. "The Community Health Aide," *Mental Hygiene*, LIII, 1 (January, 1969), 78-83.

Hamberg, Joseph. "Core Curriculum in Allied Health Education," *Journal of the American Medical Association*, CCX, 1 (October 6, 1969), 111-13.

Harden, Robert L., and John A. Monkman. "Development and Utilization of Indigenous Experts," *American Journal of Orthopsychiatry*, XLI, 2 (March, 1971), 234-36.

Harding, A. C. "How Teacher Aides Feel About Their Jobs," *National Education Association Journal*, LVI, 8 (November, 1967), 17-19.

Harrison, Bennett. "Public Employment and the Disadvantaged—Public Service Jobs for Urban Ghetto Residents," *Good Government*, LXXXVI, 3 (Fall, 1969), 1-20.

Hartley, James R. *Final Report: New Careers for Non-Professionals in Education*. Riverside: University of California Extension, 1965.

Hartog, Joseph. "A Classification of Mental Health Non-Professionals," *Mental Hygiene*, LI, 4 (October, 1967), 517-23.

Harvey, Charles E. "The Rehabilitation Aide in an Iowa Labor Union," *Rehabilitation Record*, IX, 2 (March-April, 1968), 33-35.

Harvey, L. V. "The Use of Non-Professional Auxiliary Counselors in Staffing a Counseling Service," *Journal of Counseling Psychology*, XI, 4 (Winter, 1964), 348-51.

Haskell, Mark. *The New Careers Concept: Potential for Public Employment of the Poor*. New York: Praeger, 1969.

Haynes, M. Alfred, "Professionals and Community Change," *American Journal of Public Health*, LX, 3 (March, 1970), 519-23.

"The Health Advocate," *Comprehensive Health Services and Career Development Technical Assistance Bulletin*, I, 6 (April, 1970), 1-8.

The Health Educator Aide Program for Ghetto Areas. Cincinnati: Consumer Protection and Environmental Health Service, U.S. Department of Health, Education, and Welfare, 1968.

Health Manpower Perspective, 1967. Washington, D.C.: Bureau of Health Manpower, Public Health Service, U.S. Department of Health, Education, and Welfare, 1967.

"Health Services for the Poor," *Public Health Reports*, LXXXIV, 3 (March, 1969), 192-99.

Heath, A. M. "Health Aides in Health Departments," *Public Health Report*, LXXXII, 7 (July, 1967), 608-14.

Helfer, Ray E. "A Plan for Protection: The Child Abuse Center," *Child Welfare*, XLIX, 9 (November, 1970), 486-94.

Heppner, Harry L. "Aides ... A Boon, A Blessing, An 'Open Sesame' ", *California Teachers Association Journal*, LXV, 2 (March, 1969), 39-43.

Herman, Wayne L. "Teacher Aides: How They Can Be of Real Help," *Grade Teacher*, LXXXIV, 6 (February, 1967), 102-3.

Heyman, M. M. "A Study of Effective Utilization of Social Workers in Hospital Setting," *Social Work*, VI, 2 (April, 1966), 36-43.

Hill, Julia H. "Expanding Teaching Time and Talents," *School and Community*, LV, 2 (October, 1968), 24-25.

Hoff, Wilbur. "Role of the Community Health Aide in Public Health Programs," *Public Health Reports*, LXXXIV, 11 (November, 1969), 998-1002.

―――. "Training the Disadvantaged as Home Health Aides," *Public Health Reports*, LXXXIV, 7 (July, 1969), 617-23.

―――. "Why Health Programs Are Not Reaching the Unresponsive in Our Communities," *Public Health Reports*, LXXXI, 7 (July, 1966), 654-57.

―――, *et al. Home Health Aide Pilot Training Project: Final Evaluation Report.* Oakland, Cal.: Alameda County Health Department, 1967.

Holahan, John F. *A Benefit-Cost Analysis of Project Crossroads.* Washington, D.C.: National Committee for Children and Youth, 1970.

Holzberg, James D., *et al*. "Chronic Patients and a College Companion Program," *Mental Hospitals*, XV, 3 (March, 1964), 152-58.

Home Health Aide Demonstration: Project Evaluation. New York: Daniel Yankelovich, Inc., 1967.

Houston, Laura Pires. "Black People, New Careers and Humane Human Services," *Social Casework*, LI, 5 (May, 1970), 291-99.

"How the Profession Feels About Teacher Aides," *National Education Association Journal*, LVI, 11 (November, 1967), 16-17.

Howe, Harold. *The People Who Serve Education: A Report on the State of the Education Professions by the U.S. Commissioner of Education, 1968*. Washington, D.C.: U.S. Department of Health, Education, and Welfare, 1968.

Huessy, Hans H., *et al*. "The Indigenous Nurse as Crisis Counselor and Intervenor," *American Journal of Public Health*, LIX, 11 (November, 1969), 2022-28.

Institute for Local Self-Government. "A New Careers Evaluation." Oakland: The Institute, 1969.

————. *Public Service Employment and the Disadvantaged*. Berkeley, Cal.: The Institute, 1970.

————. *Some Who Dared: Community College Programs for Public Service Occupations*. Berkeley, Cal.: The Institute, 1970.

Institute for Youth Studies, *Techniques for the Evaluation of Training Programs*. Washington, D.C.: The Institute, 1966.

"An Interim Evaluation of the Community Relations Aides' Performance in the Community Relations Program." Los Angeles: Los Angeles Police Department, 1969.

Ireland, V. M. *Evaluation of the Teacher Aide Program*. Atlanta: Atlanta Public Schools, 1969.

Jacobson, Lee. "New Careers," *Training in Business and Industry*, VII, 8 (August, 1970), 24-33.

Jacobson, Sally Lindover. "The Neighborhood Service Center of Lincoln Hospital Mental Health Services: Some Implications for Change." Speech at the National Conference of Social Welfare, Chicago, May, 1966.

Jennings, John F. "Legislation Affecting Auxiliary Personnel," *Journal of Home Economics*, LXII, 2 (February, 1970), 91-95.

Johnson, Cornelia T. "Paraprofessionals Bridging the Gap " *American Journal of Orthopsychiatry*, XLI, 2 (March, 1971), 234-35.

Jones, Betty Lacy. "Nonprofessional Workers in Professional Foster Family Agencies," *Child Welfare*, XLV, 6 (June, 1966), 313-25.

Joyce, Bruce R. *The Teacher and His Staff: Man, Media, and Machines*. Washington, D.C.: National Commission on Teacher Education and Professional Standards, National Education Association, 1967.

Keefe, John E. "Paraprofessionals: Get Them When You Need Them," *School Management*, XIII, 2 (February, 1969), 47-50.

Kent, James A., and Harvey L. Smith. "Involving the Urban Poor in Health Services Through Accommodation—The Employment of Neighborhood Representatives," *American Journal of Public Health*, LVII, 6 (June, 1967), 997-1003.

Keyserling, Leon K. *Achieving Nationwide Excellence: A Ten Year Plan, 1967-77, to Save the Schools*. Washington, D.C.: Conference on Economic Progress, 1968.

Klerman, Gerald L. "Mental Health and the Urban Crisis," *American Journal of Orthopsychiatry*, XXXIX, 5 (October, 1969), 818-26.

Klopf, Gordon J., *et al. A Learning Team: Teacher and Auxiliary*. New York: Bank Street College of Education, 1969.

Knop, Edward, *et al.* "New Careerists in Higher Education." Minneapolis: New Careers Research, University of Minnesota, 1969. Mimeographed.

Kobrin, Solomon. "The Chicago Area Project: A Twenty-Five-Year Assessment," *Annals of the American Academy of Political and Social Science*, CCCXLI (March, 1959), 19-29.

Kreitzer, S. F. "The Therapeutic Use of Volunteer Students." *Psychotherapeutic Agents: New Roles for Nonprofessionals, Parents, and Teachers*. Edited by Bernard F. Guerney, Jr. New York: Holt, Rinehart, and Winston, 1969.

Kurzman, Paul A. "The New Careers Movement and Social Change," *Social Casework*, LI, 1 (January, 1970), 22-27.

Lamb, Linda. "The Community Health Aide: A New Kind of Health Worker." Paper presented at the American Public Health Association, Annual Meeting, Philadelphia, November 12, 1969.

Lanza, Leonard G. "Paraprofessional School Aides Bridge a Social Gap," *School Management*, XIII, 2 (February, 1963), 47-52.

Larson, Patricia. "Discussions with New Careerists." Minneapolis: New Careers Research, University of Minnesota, 1969.

————. "A Functional Model for the Use of Paraprofessional Personnel." Minneapolis: New Careers Research, University of Minnesota, 1968.

————, Nancye Belding, and R. Frank Falk. "A Critique of Agencies in the Minneapolis New Careers Program." Minneapolis: New Careers Research, University of Minnesota, 1968.

————, Mary Bible, and R. Frank Falk. "Down the Up Staircase: A Study of New Careers Dropouts." Minneapolis: New Careers Research, University of Minnesota, 1969.

Lashof, Joyce C. "Chicago Project Provides Health Care and Career Opportunities," *Journal of the American Hospital Association*, XLIII, 13 (July 1, 1969), 105-8.

Leep, Albert G., and Frank Creason. "Teenage Teacher-Aide Project," *The National Elementary Principal*, XLVI, 6 (May, 1967), 45-48.

Lehman, Stanley, *et al*. "Study of Neighborhood Centers and Mental Health Aides." New York: Lincoln Hospital Mental Health Center, 1967.

Lenzer, Anthony. "New Health Careers for the Poor," *American Journal of Public Health*, LX, 1 (January, 1970), 45-50.

Letourneau, Charles. "The Assistant Physician," *Hospital Management*, CV, 4 (April, 1968), 55-57.

Levine, David L. "Intervention in the Cycle of Health Problems in the Inner City: The Role and Processes of the Family Health Worker as a Professional," *American Journal of Orthopsychiatry*, XL, 2 (March, 1970), 298-99.

Levinson, Perry, and Jeffrey Schiller. "Role Analysis of the Indigenous Nonprofessional," *Social Work*, XI, 3 (July, 1966), 97-102.

Lieberg, Leon G. *Project Crossroads: A Final Report to the Manpower Administration, U.S. Department of Labor*. Washington, D.C.: National Committee on Children and Youth, 1971.

Liebert, Lisa. "Police-Community Relations and the Role of the Nonprofessional." New York: New Careers Development Center, New York University, 1968.

Lief, Harold I. "Subprofessional Training in Mental Health," *Archives of General Psychiatry*, XV, 6 (December, 1966), 660-64.

Light, Israel. "Development and Growth of New Allied Health Fields," *Journal of the American Medical Association*, CCX, 1 (October 6, 1969), 114-210.

Loewenberg, Fred M. "Social Workers and Indigenous Nonprofessionals: Some Structural Dilemmas," *Social Work*, XIII, 3 (July, 1968), 65-71.

Lowery, Patti L., and William H. Denham. *New Careers: Paraprofessional Personnel in Public Education*. Washington, D.C.: National Institute for New Careers, University Research Corporation, 1970.

Luckham, Jane, and David W. Swift. "Community Health Aides in the Ghetto: The Contra Costa Project." Unpublished Ms., Richmond, Cal., 1968.

Lynch, Mary, *et al*. "The Role of Indigenous Personnel as Clinical Therapists," *Archives of General Psychiatry*, XIX, 4 (October, 1968), 428-34.

Lynton, Edith F. "The Nonprofessional Scene," *American Child*, XLIX, 1 (Winter, 1967), 9-13.

_____. *The Subprofessional: From Concepts to Careers*. New York: National Committee on Employment of Youth, 1967.

Macfarlane, Ruth. "New Careers in Action," *Educational Leadership*, XXVIII, 4 (January, 1971), 351-54.

MacLennan, Beryce W. "New Careers as Human Service Aides," *Children*, XIII, 5 (September-October, 1966), 190-94.

_____, and William L. Klein. "Utilization of Groups in Job Training for the Socially Deprived," *International Journal of Group Psychology*, XV, 4 (October, 1965), 424-33.

Malamud, Irene T. "Volunteers in Community Mental Health Work," *Mental Hygiene*, XXXIX, 2 (April, 1965), 300-9.

The Manhattan Court Employment Project of the Vera Institute of Justice, Summary Report on Phase One: November 1, 1967 to October 3, 1969. New York: Vera Institute of Justice, 1970.

Martens, E. G., and S. N. Ryoner. "Health Education for 200,000 Canadians," *Health Educators at Work*. Edited by E. S. Tyler and L. S. Morgan. Chapel Hill: University of North Carolina, 1964.

Mary Alice, Sister, and Adma D'Heule. "New Ventures in School Organization—The Ungraded School and Use of Teacher Aides," *The Elementary School Journal*, LVII, 6 (February, 1957), 288-91.

Massimo, J. L., and M. F. Shore. "Effectiveness of a Comprehensive Vocationally Oriented Therapeutic Program for Adolescent Boys," *American Journal of Orthopsychiatry*, XXXIII, 6 (June, 1963), 634-42.

Matheny, Kenneth B., and Yvonne Oslin. "Utilization of Paraprofessionals in Education and the Helping Professions: A Review of the Literature." Paper presented to the American Educational Research Association, Minneapolis, March, 1970.

Maves, Harold J. "The Community Enters the Classroom," *California Teachers Association Journal*, LXV, 2 (March, 1969), 26-28.

Mental Health Worker Career Series. Springfield, Ill.: Department of Mental Health, 1970.

Millman, Linda, and Catherine S. Chilman. *Poor People at Work: An Annotated Bibliography on Semi-Professionals in Education, Health, and Welfare Services.* Washington, D.C.: Intramural Research Division, Office of Research, Demonstration and Training, Social and Rehabilitation Service, U.S. Department of Health, Education, and Welfare, n.d.

Minuchin, Salvador. "The Paraprofessional and the Use of Confrontation in the Mental Health Field," *American Journal of Orthopsychiatry*, XXXIX, 5 (October, 1969), 722-29.

Misner, Gordon E., and Wendell Jones. "Police Careers." *Up From Poverty: New Career Ladders for Nonprofessionals.* Edited by Frank Riessman and Hermine I. Popper. New York: Harper and Row, 1968.

Mitchell, Lonnie E., *et al.* "Baker's Dozen: A Program for Training Young People as Mental Health Aides." *Mental Health Program Reports.* Washington, D.C.: National Institute for Mental Health, II (1968), 11-24.

————. *Training for Community Mental Health Aides: Leaders for Child and Adolescent Therapeutic Activity Groups: Report of a Program.* Washington, D.C.: Institute for Youth Studies, Howard University, 1966.

Mitchell, William E. "Amica Therapy: Theoretical Perspectives and an Example of Practice," *Community Mental Health Journal*, II, 4 (Winter, 1966), 307-14.

Montgomery, Helen B. "Differential Utilization of Social Work Personnel," *Children*, XI, 3 (May-June, 1964), 103-7.

Mood, Alexander. *Do Teachers Make a Difference? A Report on Recent Research on Pupil Achievement.* Washington, D.C.: U.S. Office of Education, 1970.

Morrison, Andrew P. "Consultation and Group Processes with Indigenous Neighborhood Workers," *Community Mental Health Journal*, VI, 1 (February, 1970), 3-12.

Murphy, Lois Barclay, *et al.* "A Psychotherapeutic Aide in a Headstart Program," *Children*, XVI, 1 (January-February, 1969), 18-22.

National Committee on Employment for Youth. *The CAP Aide Study.* New York, 1966.

_____. *Career Mobility for Paraprofessionals in Human Service Agencies.* Washington, D.C.: U.S. Department of Labor, 1969.

_____. *Opportunity or Deadend: The Future for CAP Aides, Final Report of the CAP Aide Study.* New York, 1966.

National Institute for New Careers. *An Assessment of Technical Assistance and Training Needs in New Careers Projects Being Sponsored by the United States Training and Employment Service, Manpower Administration, U.S. Department of Labor.* Washington, D.C.: University Research Corporation, 1969.

_____. *The Community Home Health Aide.* Washington, D.C.: University Research Corporation, 1968.

_____. *Generic Issues of the Human Services: A Sourcebook for Trainers.* Washington, D.C.: University Research Corporation, 1968.

_____. *New Careers Bibliography: Paraprofessionals in the Human Services.* Washington, D.C.: University Research Corporation, 1970.

_____. *New Careers in Health: A Status Report.* Washington, D.C.: University Research Corporation, 1970.

_____. *New Careers in Mental Health: A Status Report.* Washington, D.C.: University Research Corporation, 1970.

_____. *New Careers in Social Welfare: A Status Report.* Washington, D.C.: University Research Corporation, 1970.

_____. *The Social Service Aide: A Manual for Trainers.* Washington, D.C.: University Research Corporation, 1968.

_____. *The Social Service Aide: A Sourcebook for Trainers.* Washington, D.C.: University Research Corporation, 1968.

_____. *The Teacher Aide: A Manual for Trainees.* Washington, D.C.: University Research Corporation, 1968.

National League of Cities. *Municipal Government Efforts to Provide Career Employment Opportunities for the Disadvantaged.* Washington, D.C., 1970.

National Manpower Task Force. *Conference on Upgrading and New Careers.* Washington, D.C., 1970.

Nelson, Gaylord. "S.271, Teacher Aide Program Support Act of 1967," *The National Elementary Principal,* XLVI, 6 (May, 1967), 40-44.

Nestig, Gordon. "Testimony Presented Before the U.S. Senate Labor Committee, Sub-Committee on Manpower." Los Angeles, January 7, 1970.

Neugeboren, Bernard. "New Haven's Unified Social Service Project." New Brunswick, N.J.: Rutgers, the State University, 1968.

New Careers and HEW. Washington, D.C.: U.S. Department of Health, Education, and Welfare, 1970.

New Careers Development Center. *New Careers, 1968-69, A Report to the Ford Foundation.* New York: New York University, 1969.

New Careers in Teaching: Differentiated Staffing. Temple City, Cal.: Temple City Unified School District, 1969.

"New Health Occupations Program." New York: Mobilization for Youth, 1968.

Newlin, Wayne. "It Can Be Done: Teacher Aides Can Make a Difference in Illinois." *Illinois Education,* LVI, 5 (January, 1968), 213-16.

Newman, Howard N. "Community Leaders Can Help Deliver Services to the Poor," *Journal of the American Hospital Association,* XLIII, 3 (July 1, 1969), 63-66.

Newman, Leonard. "Instant Placement: A New Model for Providing Rehabilitation Services Within a Community Mental Health Program," *Community Mental Health Journal,* VI, 5 (October, 1970), 401-10.

Nixon, R. A. *Legislative Dimensions of the New Careers Program: 1970.* New York: Center for the Study of the Unemployed, New York University, 1970.

Noar, Gertrude. *Teacher Aides at Work.* Washington, D.C.: National Commission on Teacher Education and Professional Standards, National Education Association, 1967.

Olivero, James L. "Do Teacher Aides Really Aid?" *California Teachers Association Journal*, LXV, 2 (March, 1969), 34-38.

Olson, Irene, "Junior College Education for Social Service Assistant," *Child Welfare*, XLV, 10 (December, 1966), 599-600.

Park, Charles B. "The Bay City Experiment . . . As Seen by the Director," *Journal of Teacher Education*, VII, 2 (June, 1956), 101-10.

Parker, Glenn M., and Barry A. Passett. "The Poor Bring Adult Education to the Ghetto," *Adult Leadership*, VI, 9 (March, 1969), 327-48.

Patterson, Patricia K., *et al.* "Parent Reaction to the Concept of Pediatric Assistants," *Pediatrics*, XLIV, 1 (July, 1969), 72-78.

Pearl, Arthur, "An Address at the Planning Conference on New Careers," Kansas City, Missouri, 1967.

————, and Frank Riessman. *New Careers for the Poor: The Nonprofessional in Human Service.* New York: Free Press, 1965.

The People Who Serve Education: A Report on the State of the Education Professions. Washington, D.C.: Office of Education, U.S. Department of Health, Education, and Welfare, 1969.

Perry, J. Warren. "Career Mobility in Allied Health Education," *Journal of the American Medical Association*, CCX, 1 (October 6, 1969), 107-10.

Piemer, Sidney C., *et al.* "An Experiment in Retraining Unemployed Men for Practical Nursing Careers," *Journal of the American Hospital Association*, XL, 20 (October 16, 1966), 87-91.

Pilnick, Sol, *et al.* "The Essexfields Concept, A New Approach to the Social Treatment of Juvenile Delinquents," *Journal of Applied Behavioral Research*, II, 1 (January, 1966), 109-25.

Pines, Maya. "The Coming Upheaval in Psychiatry," *Harper's Magazine* (October, 1965), 1-7.

Pope, Lillian. "Blueprint for a Successful Paraprofessional Tutorial Program," *American Journal of Orthopsychiatry*, XL, 2 (March, 1970), 299-300.

Potts, D., and C. W. Miller. "The Community Health Aide," *Nursing Outlook*, XII, 12 (December, 1964), 33-35.

Powell, Rodney N. "MEDEX: A Breakthrough in Medicine," *Hospital Tribune*, IV, 4 (September 21, 1970), 278-82.

Ohio Education Association, *Educational Aides,* Research Bulletin, No. 5. Columbus, 1970.

Powledge, Fred. *New Careers: Real Jobs and Opportunities for the Disadvantaged.* "Public Affairs Pamphlet," No. 427. New York, 1968.

Programmed Tutoring Follow-Up. Muncie: The Reading Center, School of Education, University of Indiana, 1969.

"Providing Vocational Rehabilitation Services in Sparsely Settled Areas of Wyoming." Cheyenne: Final Report, The Wyoming Aide Project, Division of Vocational Rehabilitation, State Department of Education, 1969.

Pruger, Robert, and Harry Specht. "Establishing New Careers Programs: Organizational Barriers and Strategies," *Social Work,* XIII, 4 (October, 1968), 21-32.

Public Education in New York City. New York: First National City Bank, 1969.

Public Service Jobs for Urban Ghetto Residents. Washington, D.C.: National Civil Service League, 1969.

Rademacher, Elizabeth. *A Training Program for Teacher Aides.* Eugene: University of Oregon, 1968.

Rand, M. John. "A Case for Differentiated Staff," *California Teachers Association Journal,* LXV, 2 (March, 1969), 29-33.

Reichler, Robert J., *et al.* "The Mental Health Team: A Model for a Combined Community Approach to the Problems of the Poor," *American Journal of Orthopsychiatry,* XXXVI, 3 (April, 1966), 434-43.

Reiff, Robert, and Frank Riessman. *The Indigenous Nonprofessional: A Strategy of Change in Community Action and Community Mental Health Programs.* New York: National Institute of Labor Education, 1964.

Reiser, Martin, and Zanwil Sperber. "Utilizing Nonprofessional Case Aides in the Treatment of Psychotic Children of an Outpatient Clinic," *American Journal of Orthopsychiatry,* XXXIX, 2 (March, 1969), 356-57.

"Report to the U.S. Office of Economic Opportunity on the South Bronx Neighborhood Service Center Program." December, 1965.

Rhode Island State Department of Education. *Auxiliary School Personnel: Their Employment and Utilization.* Providence, 1969.

Richan, W. L. "A Theoretical Scheme for Determining Roles of Professional and Nonprofessional Personnel," *Social Work*, VI, 4 (October, 1961), 22-28.

Ridenour, Lenore Karpelowsky. "The Rehabilitation Aide in Watts and Nearby Neighborhoods," *Rehabilitation Record*, IX, 2 (March-April, 1968), 38-40.

Riedesel, Mildred, and Harriet Johnston. "Agawes of Chippewas," *Journal of Home Economics*, LXII, 2 (February, 1970), 120-22.

Riessman, Frank. "The 'Helper-Therapy' Principle," *Social Work*, X, 2 (April, 1965), 27-32.

_____. "Memorandum to Representative James Scheuer." March 7, 1966.

_____. "A Neighborhood-Based Mental Health Approach." *Emergent Approaches to Mental Health Problems.* Edited by Emory L. Cowen *et al.* New York: Appleton-Century-Crofts, 1967.

_____. "The Neighborhood Service Center: An Innovation in Preventive Psychiatry," *American Journal of Psychiatry*, CXXIII, 11 (May, 1967), 184-92.

_____. "The New Careers Concept," *American Child*, XLIX, 1 (Winter, 1967), 2-8.

_____. "New Interventions for Disadvantaged Youth," *American Journal of Orthopsychiatry*, CXXIII, 7 (January, 1967), 880-82.

_____. "The Revolution in Social Work: The New Nonprofessional," *Trans-Action*, II, 1 (November-December, 1964), 12-17.

_____. "The Revolution in Social Work: The New Nonprofessional." New York: Mobilization for Youth, 1963.

_____, and Emanuel Hallowitz. "Neighborhood Service Center Program." A Report to the U.S. Office of Economic Opportunity on the South Bronx Neighborhood Service Center, December, 1965.

_____, and Hermine I. Popper, *Up From Poverty: New Career Ladders for Nonprofessionals.* New York: Harper and Row, 1968.

Rioch, Margaret J. "Changing Concepts in the Training of Therapists," *Journal of Counselling Psychology*, XXX, 4 (August, 1966), 290-92.

————, *et al.* "National Institute of Mental Health Pilot Study in Training Mental Health Counselors," *American Journal of Orthopsychiatry,* XXXIII 4 (July, 1963), 678-89.

Rioux, J. William. "Here are Fourteen Ways to Use Nonteachers in Your School District," *Nation's Schools,* LXXVI, 6 (December, 1965), 42.

Rittenhouse, Carl G. *An Interpretive Study of the Use of Paraprofessional Aides in Education.* Menlo Park, Cal.: Stanford Research Institute, 1969.

Roberts, B. J., *et al.* "An Experimental Study of Two Approaches to Communicate," *American Journal of Public Health,* LIII, (September, 1963), 1361-81.

Roman, Melvin, *et al.* "Teaching of Community Mental Health Worker." New York: Lincoln Hospital Mental Health Services, 1967.

Rooner-Pieczenic, Roberta. *Project Crossroads as Pre-Trial Intervention: A Program Evaluation.* Washington, D.C.: National Committee for Children and Youth, 1970.

Rosenbaum, Max. "Some Comments on the Use of Untrained Therapists," *Journal of Counselling Psychology,* XXX, 4 (August, 1966), 292-94.

Saltzman, Henry. "The Poor and the Schools." *New Careers for the Poor: The Nonprofessional in Human Service.* Arthur Pearl and Frank Riessman. New York: Free Press, 1965.

Sarwin, James Donald. "Criteria for Statutory Provisions for the Employment of Teacher Aides in Public School Districts." Unpublished Ph.D. dissertation, University of Colorado, 1969.

Schmais, Aaron. *Implementing Nonprofessional Programs in Human Services.* New York: Graduate School of Social Work, New York University, 1967.

Schmidt, Lyle D. "Comment on 'Differential Functioning of Lay and Professional Helpers' ", *Journal of Counselling Psychology,* XV, 2 (March, 1968), 127-29.

Schorr, Lisbeth Bamburger, and Joseph T. English. "Background, Context and Significant Issues in Neighborhood Health Center Programs," *The Millbank Memorial Fund Quarterly,* XLVI, 3 Pt. I (July, 1968), 289-96.

Scrivner, A. W. and R. Urbanek. "The Value of 'Teacher-Aide' Participation in the Elementary School," *The Arithmetic Teacher,* X, 2 (February, 1963), 84-87.

Serving More Disabled Better Through New Careers in Rehabilitation. Washington, D.C.: National Rehabilitation Assocation, n.d.

Shank, Paul C., and Wayne R. McElroy. *The Paraprofessionals.* Midland, Mich.: Pendell Publishing Co., 1970.

"Shared Experiences: From Professionals and Auxiliary Personnel," *Journal of Home Economics,* LXII, 2 (February, 1970), 109-13.

Sheppard, Harold L. *The Nature of the Job Problem and the Role of Public Service Employment.* Kalamazoo, Mich.: W. E. Upjohn Institute, 1969.

Shipp, Mary D. "Teacher Aides: A Survey," *National Elementary Principal,* XLVI, 6 (May, 1967), 30-33.

Silver, H. K. "The Use of New Types of Allied Health Professions in Providing Care for Children," *American Journal of Diseases of Children,* CXVI, 11 (November, 1968), 486-90.

_____, *et al.* "Pediatric Nurse-Practitioner Program," *Journal of the American Medical Association,* CCIV, 4 (April 22, 1968), 298-302.

Singer, Ira J. "Survey of Staff Utilization Practices in Six States," *National Association of Secondary School Principals Bulletin,* XLVI, 270 (January, 1962), 1-11.

Sinnett, T. M. *A Manual on Certification Requirements for School Personnel in the United States, 1970 Edition.* Washington, D.C.: National Education Association, 1970.

Smith, M. Brewster, and Charles Hobbs. "The Community and the Community Mental Health Center," *American Psychologist,* XXI, 6 (June, 1966), 499-509.

Smith, Merle. "A Description of a Teacher Aide Program, 1968-1969." Pontiac, Mich.: Pontiac Public Schools, 1969.

Snyder, Fred A. "Teachers' Perception of Para-Professionals," *Contemporary Education,* XXXIV, 4 (January, 1968), 145-47.

Sobey, Francine. *The Nonprofessional Revolution in Mental Health.* New York: Columbia University Press, 1970.

Social Development Corporation. *Merit Systems: Hiring the Disadvantaged.* Washington, D.C., 1970.

_____. *New Careers Job Descriptions.* Washington, D.C., 1969.

————. *New Careers Police-Community Relations.* Washington, D.C., 1970.

"Social Health Technicians." New York: Mobilization for Youth, 1970.

"Social-Psychological Changes in New Careerists." Minneapolis: New Careers Research, University of Minnesota, 1969.

Soong, Robert K., *et al.* "Social Service Aide Project for the Education and Training of Paraprofessionals, Final Report." Chicago: YMCA of Metropolitan Chicago, Inc., 1969.

Specht, Harry, *et al.* "Case Conference on Neighborhood Subprofessional Workers," *Children,* XV, 1 (January-February, 1968), 7-16.

Staffing for Better Schools. Washington, D.C.: Office of Education, U.S. Department of Health, Education, and Welfare, 1967.

Starie, John H., and Margaret Stevenson. "Local Associations Ask About Paraprofessionals," *National Education Association Journal,* LVI, 6 (September, 1967), 74.

State Department of Public Instruction. *Suggested Guidelines for Utilizing Supplementary Educational Personnel.* Phoenix, Ariz., 1970.

Stead, E. A., Jr. "Conserving Costly Talents—Providing Physicians' Assistants," *Journal of the American Medical Association,* XCVIII, 12 (December 5, 1966), 1108-09.

————. "The Duke Plan for Physicians' Assistants," *Medical Times,* XCV, 1 (January, 1967), 40-48.

————. "Training and Use of Paramedical Personnel," *New England Journal of Medicine,* CCLXXVII, 10 (October, 1967), 800-1.

Stein, Francine, "New Careers in Family Planning," *Family Planning Perspectives,* I, 2 (October, 1969), 42-44.

Steinberg, Sheldon S. "Stresses, Strains, and Joys of Utilizing Auxiliary Personnel," *Journal of Home Economics,* LXII, 2 (February, 1970), 96-102.

————, *et al.* "New Careers: A Major Solution to the Environmental Health Problem," *American Journal of Public Health,* LIX, 7 (July, 1969), 1118-23.

Stewart, James Carl. "Employment of Indigenous Personnel as a Strategy for Increasing Immunization Rates in 'Hard Core' Areas." Unpublished Ph.D. dissertation, University of Oklahoma, n.d.

A Study of Selected Programs for the Education of Disadvantaged Children. Palo Alto, Cal.: American Institute for Research, 1968.

"A Symposium: The Bay City, Michigan Experiment, A Cooperative Study for the Better Utilization of Teacher Competencies," *Journal of Teacher Education,* VII, 2 (June, 1956), 110-52.

Tanner, Daniel and Laurel N. Tanner. "Teacher Aides, A Job for Anyone in Ghetto Schools," *The Record,* LXIX, 8 (May, 1968), 743-51.

TAP: The Teacher Aide Program. Washington, D.C.: Washington School of Psychiatry, 1967.

Teacher Aide Program, 1966-67. Minneapolis: Minneapolis Public Schools, 1967.

"Teacher Aides," *School and Society,* XCV, 2286 (January 21, 1967), 38-39.

Teacher Aides: A Status Report. Terre Haute: School of Education, Indiana State University, 1968.

"Teacher Aides in Large School Systems." Washington, D.C.: Research Division, National Education Association, 1967.

"Teacher Aides in the Public Schools." *National Education Association Research Bulletin,* XLV, 2 (May, 1967), 37-39; XLVIII, 1 (March, 1970), 11-12.

The Teacher and His Staff. Grand Forks, N.D.: Grand Forks School District, 1969.

The Teacher and His Staff: Differentiating Teaching Roles. Washington, D.C.: National Commission on Teacher Education and Professional Standards, National Education Association, 1969.

Thompson, Margaret A. "Contamination of New Careerists by Professionalization: Fact or Fancy?" Minneapolis: New Careers Research, University of Minnesota, 1969.

_____. "The Minneapolis New Careers Program: A Follow-Up Study." Minneapolis: Office of Career Development, University of Minnesota, 1971.

_____. "The New Careerist: A Description." Minneapolis: New Careers Research, University of Minnesota, 1969.

_____, *et al.* "Job Interests and Job Satisfactions of New Careerists." Minneapolis: New Careers Research, University of Minnesota, 1969.

Toward a Career Ladder in Nursing: Upgrading Nurse's Aides to LPNs Through a Work-Study Program, Final Progress Report. New York, 1970.

Townsend, E. H. "Paramedical Personnel in Pediatric Practice," *Journal of Pediatrics,* LVIII, 6 (June, 1966), 855-59.

Training and Supervision of New Careerists in Rehabilitation. Washington, D.C.: National Rehabilitation Association, n.d.

"Training of Community Mental Health Workers, July 1, 1966-June 30, 1967." New York: Lincoln Hospital Mental Health Services, 1967.

"A Training Program for Teacher Aides." *Up From Poverty: New Career Ladders for Nonprofessionals.* Edited by Frank Riessman and Hermine I. Popper. New York: Harper and Row, 1968.

Trebach, Arnold, and Evelyn Idelson. *New Careers in Justice: A Status Report.* Washington, D.C.: National Institute for New Careers, 1970.

Truax, Charles B. "An Approach Toward Training for the Aide-Therapist: Research and Implications." Fayetteville: Arkansas Rehabilitation Research and Training Center, 1965.

————. "The Use of Supportive Personnel in Rehabilitation Counselling." Fayetteville: Arkansas Rehabilitation Research and Training Center, n.d.

————, and James L. Lister. "Effectiveness of Counselors and Counselor Aides," *Journal of Counselling Psychology,* XVII, 4 (July, 1970), 331-34.

Trump, J. L. "A Look Ahead in Secondary Education," *National Association of Secondary School Principals Bulletin,* XLII, 234 (January, 1958), 5-15.

"Up the Up Staircase: Impressions of the New Careerist as Student." Minneapolis: Office of New Careers, University of Minnesota, 1969.

Urvant, Penny. "Health Advocates," *Public Health Reports,* LXXXIV, 9 (September, 1969), 761-66.

The Use Of Teacher Aides in Colorado. Denver: Colorado Department of Education, 1968.

"Use of Teacher Aides, 1968-69." Washington, D.C.: Research Memo 1969-11, National Education Association, 1969.

Utilization of Paraprofessional Personnel in Intensive Remedial Reading, End of Project Report. Hammond, Ind.: City of Hammond Schools, 1970.

Vanderpool, Alden. "California's Instructional Aide Act," *California Teachers Journal,* LXV, 2 (March, 1969), 5.

Vera Institute of Justice. *The Manhattan Court Employment Project, Phase I.* New York, 1970.

Vidaver, Robert M. "The Mental Health Technician: Maryland's Design for a New Health Career," *American Journal of Psychiatry,* CXXV, 8 (February, 1969), 1013-23.

Vogel, Anita. *Establishing a New Career: The Social Health Technician.* New York: Mobilization for Youth, 1970.

Wade, Ruth, *et al.* "The View of the Paraprofessional," *American Journal of Orthopsychiatry,* XXXIX, 4 (July, 1969), 677-83.

Walker, Walter L., and Lonnie E. Mitchell. "Group Decision-Making in an Apprenticeship Program for Youth," *American Journal of Orthopsychiatry,* XXXVII, 1 (January, 1967), 101-6.

Wallace, Hilda. "The Paraprofessional Mental Health Workers: What Are We All About?" *American Journal of Orthopsychiatry,* XL, 2 (March, 1970), 296-97.

Ward, Eric J. "A Gift from the Ghetto," *The Personnel and Guidance Journal,* XLVIII, 9 (May, 1970), 753-56.

Weber, George H., and Diane Palmer. "New Careers Problems and Pitfalls," *American Education,* V, 4 (April, 1969), 26-28.

Weed, Verne, and William H. Denham. "Toward More Effective Use of the Nonprofessional Worker: A Recent Experiment," *Social Work,* VI, 4 (October, 1961), 29-36.

Weisz, Vera C. *A Junior College's Approach to Training Auxiliary Personnel In Education.* Boston: Garland Junior College, 1968.

Wellner, Alfred M., and Ralph Simon. "A Survey of Associate Degree Programs for Mental Health Technicians," *Hospitals and Community Psychiatry,* XX, 6 (June, 1969), 166-69.

White, Richardson, Jr., and John H. Stein. *Paraprofessionals in Legal Service Programs: A Feasibility Study.* Washington, D.C.: National Institute for Justice and Law Enforcement, 1968.

Williams, Judith R., and Mark Zborowski. "The Etiology of a Children and Youth Project's Malaise," *American Journal of Public Health,* LX, 8 (August, 1970), 1398-1401.

Wilson, Jim. "Dormitory Teacher Aides Are Big Help in South Dakota," *Journal of American Indian Education,* IX, 2 (January, 1970), 3-9.

Wingert, Willis A., *et al.* "Indigenous Health Aides as Counselors to Parents About Nutrition," *Public Health Reports,* LXXXIV, 4 (April, 1969), 328-32.

Wise, Harold B. "Montefiore Hospital Neighborhood Medical Care Demonstration," *Millbank Memorial Fund Quarterly,* XLVI, 3, Pt. I (July, 1968), 297-307.

_____, *et al.* "The Family Health Worker," *American Journal of Public Health,* LVIII, 10 (October, 1968), 1828-35.

Wynn, D. Richard, and Richard W. DeRemer. "Staff Utilization, Development, and Evaluation," *Review of Education Research,* XXXI, 4 (October, 1961), 393-405.

Yankauer, Alfred, *et al.* "Task Performance and Task Delegation in Pediatric Office Practice," *American Journal of Public Health,* LIX, 7 (July, 1967), 1104-17.

Yankelovich, Daniel, Inc. *A Study of the Nonprofessional in the CAP.* New York, 1966.

Young, M. M., and Genevieve P. Hamlin. "People Workers: A Local Health Department's Experience with Health Education Aides," *American Journal of Public Health,* LIX, 10 (October, 1969), 1845-50.

Zahn, Stella. "Neighborhood Medical Care Demonstration Training Program," *Millbank Memorial Fund Quarterly,* XLVI, 3, Pt. I (July, 1968), 309-28.

Zax, Melvin, *et al.* "A Teacher-Aide Program for Preventing Emotional Disturbances in Young Schoolchildren," *Mental Hygiene,* L, 3 (July, 1966), 406-15.

Zimberg, Sheldon. "Outpatient Geriatric Psychiatry in an Urban Ghetto with Nonprofessional Workers," *American Journal of Psychiatry,* CXXV, 12 (June, 1969), 111-16.

ABOUT THE AUTHOR

Alan Gartner is Associate Director of the New Careers Development Center, New York University, where he designs and conducts studies of new careers programs, provides training and technical assistance to these programs, and edits the Center's *New Human Services Newsletter.* He has served as a special consultant to the U.S. Department of Health, Education, and Welfare, the Office of Education, the Office of Economic Opportunity, and other agencies concerned with the development, implementation, and evaluation of new careers programs. He was formerly Executive Director of the Economic Opportunity Council of Suffolk, New York, Community Relations Director of the Congress on Racial Equality, and a teacher in the Newton, Massachusetts public schools.

He is coauthor of *Children Teach Children: Learning Through Teaching,* has published articles in the *Nation, Social Work, Urban Review, New Generation,* and is Executive Editor of *Social Policy.*

Mr. Gartner received his A.B. from Antioch College and his M.A. from Harvard University.